Foundations of Finance

The Logic and Practice of Financial Management

Chapters 4 and 9

Arthur J. Keown
Virginia Polytechnic Institute and State University
R.B. Pamplin Professor of Finance

David F. Scott, Jr.
University of Central Florida
Holder, Phillips-Schenck Chair in American Private Enterprise
and Professor of Finance

John D. Martin
University of Texas at Austin
Margaret and Eugene McDermott Professor of Banking and Finance

J. William Petty
Baylor University
Caruth Professor of Entrepreneurship

SIMON & SCHUSTER CUSTOM PUBLISHING

Cover design: Felicity Erwin

Excerpts taken from:
Foundations of Finance: The Logic and Practice of Financial Management,
by Arthur J. Keown, David F. Scott, Jr., John D. Martin, and J. William Petty
Copyright © 1994 by Prentice-Hall, Inc.
Simon & Schuster Company / A Viacom Company
Upper Saddle River, New Jersey 07458

This special edition published in cooperation with
Simon & Schuster Custom Publishing

Printed in the United States of America

10 9 8 7 6 5 4 3 2

Please visit our website at www.sscp.com

ISBN 0–536–00721–7

BA 98244

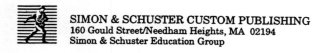

SIMON & SCHUSTER CUSTOM PUBLISHING
160 Gould Street/Needham Heights, MA 02194
Simon & Schuster Education Group

Table of Contents

CHAPTER 4
FINANCIAL FORECASTING, PLANNING, AND BUDGETING

Financial Forecasting • Financial Planning and Budgeting
• Computerized Financial Planning

The impact of computers and financial software on the practice of financial forecasting, planning, and budgeting has been dramatic. Financial spreadsheet programs allow the financial analyst to tabulate very large and cumbersome budgets, which, with the aid of a microcomputer, can then be easily modified to reflect any number of possible scenarios. This type of "trial-and-error" analysis can greatly enhance analysts' decision-making capability by allowing them to quickly and easily assess the importance of the projections and assumptions that go into any financial plan.

This chapter has two primary objectives: First, it will develop an appreciation for the role of forecasting in the firm's financial planning process. Basically, forecasts of future sales revenues and their associated expenses give the firm the information needed to project its future needs for financing. Second, the chapter will provide an overview of the firm's budgetary system, including the cash budget and the pro forma, or planned, income statement and balance sheet. Pro forma financial statements give the financial manager a useful tool for analyzing the effects of the firm's forecasts and planned activities on its financial performance, as well as its needs for financing. In addition, pro forma statements can be used as a benchmark or standard to compare against actual operating results. Used in this way, pro forma statements are an instrument for controlling or monitoring the firm's progress throughout the planning period.

BACK TO THE FUNDAMENTALS

Financial decisions are made today in light of our expectations of an uncertain future. Financial forecasting involves making estimates of the future financing requirements of the firm. **Axiom 3: Cash Is King—Measuring the Timing of Costs and Benefits** speaks directly to this problem. Remember that effective financial management requires that consideration be given to cash flow and when it is received or dispersed.

■ FINANCIAL FORECASTING

Forecasting in financial management is used to estimate a firm's future financial needs. The basic steps involved in predicting those financing needs are the following: **Step 1:** Project the firm's sales revenues and expenses over the planning period. **Step 2:** Estimate the levels of investment in current and fixed assets that are necessary to support the projected sales. **Step 3:** Determine the firm's financing needs throughout the planning period.

Sales Forecast

The key ingredient in the firm's planning process is the **sales forecast**. This projection is generally derived using information from a number of sources. At a minimum, the sales forecast for the coming year would reflect (1) any past trend in sales that is expected to carry through into the new year and (2) the influence of any events that might materially affect that trend.[1] An example of the latter would be the initiation of a major advertising campaign or a change in the firm's pricing policy.

Forecasting Financial Variables

Traditional financial forecasting takes the sales forecast as a given and makes projections of its impact on the firm's various expenses, assets, and liabilities. The most commonly used method for making these projections is the percent of sales method.

Percent of Sales Method of Financial Forecasting

The **percent of sales method** involves estimating the level of an expense, asset, or liability for a future period as a percent of the sales forecast. The percentage used can come from the most recent financial statement item as a percent of current sales, from an average computed

---

[1] A complete discussion of forecast methodologies is outside the scope of this book. The interested reader will find the following references helpful: F. Gerard Adams, *The Business Forecasting Revolution* (Oxford: Oxford University Press, 1986); C.W.J. Granger, *Forecasting in Business and Economics*, 2d ed. (Boston, MA: Academic Press, 1989); and Paul Newbold and Theodore Bos, *Introductory Business Forecasting* (Cincinnati, OH: Southwestern, 1990).

BASIC FINANCIAL MANAGEMENT IN PRACTICE

Now You See It...

Cash flow is at least as important a measure of corporate health as reported earnings. But put a dozen investors in a room and you'll get almost as many different definitions of "cash flow" (*Forbes*, Apr. 7, 1986).

After grappling with the problem for more than six years, the Financial Accounting Standards Board has come up with the beginnings of a more precise definition. It would require all companies to use the same format to explain how cash and cash equivalents change from one reporting period to the next. The proposal still leaves companies with room for flexibility but will make investors' lives much easier. Why? Companies will have to show sources and uses of cash in three areas: operations, investing, and financing.

Let's take a specific case: Lowe's Cos., the North Carolina-based retailer of building materials. The company said in its annual report that cash flow amounted to $2.31 per share in 1985 as compared with $2.20 the year before. An investor looking at these numbers might have assumed Lowe's had plenty of cash left over for dividends and other purposes.

Not necessarily so. Although Lowe's used a generally accepted definition of cash flow, it was not a strict definition. It failed to subtract the cash absorbed by higher inventories and receivables. Lowe's ended the year with hardly more cash than it started the year, and its long-term debt almost doubled from 1984 to 1985—despite the positive cash flow.

Does it really matter how you measure cash flow? Very much. While Lowe's is healthy—the increased inventory and receivables simply reflect growth in revenues—there are situations where a company can go broke while reporting positive cash flow. How can this be? Simple.

Suppose inventories and receivables rise faster than sales, reflecting slow pay by customers and unsold goods. Under the simpler method of reporting cash flow (which would not include working-capital components), such a company could report a positive cash flow even while it was fast running out of cash.

When the smoke clears, investors will still need to do lots of homework. It's never enough to know just what the numbers are. You still have to figure out what the numbers mean. Again, Lowe's is an example. Even if it were forced to report a negative cash flow, it would still be a very healthy business; it would cease being one only if inventories and receivables increased faster than sales and the company's credit were deteriorating.

When it comes to some things, the more you try simplifying them, the more complicated they become.

Source: Tatiana Pouschine, "Now You See It .," excerpted by permission of *Forbes* magazine, February 9, 1987, page 70. © Forbes Inc. 1987.

over several years, from the judgment of the analyst, or from some combination of these sources.

Figure 4–1 presents a complete example of the use of the percent of sales method of financial forecasting. In this example each item in the firm's balance sheet that varies with sales is converted to a percentage of 1993 sales. The forecast of the new balance for each item is then calculated by multiplying this percentage times the $12 million in projected sales for the 1994 planning period. This method of forecasting future financing is not as precise or detailed as the method using a cash budget, which is presented later; however, it offers a relatively low-cost and easy-to-use first approximation of the firm's financing needs for a future period.

Note that in the example in Figure 4–1, both current and fixed assets are assumed to vary with the level of firm sales. This means that

FINANCIAL FORECASTING,
PLANNING,
AND BUDGETING

Assets	Present (1993)	Percent of Sales (1993 Sales = $10 M)	Projected (Based on 1994 Sales = $12 M)
Current assets	$2.0 M	$\frac{\$2\,M}{\$10\,M} = 20\%$	$.2 \times \$12\,M = \$2.4\,M$
Net fixed assets	4.0 M	$\frac{\$4\,M}{\$10\,M} = 40\%$	$.4 \times \$12\,M = 4.8\,M$
Total	$6.0 M		$7.2 M
Liabilities and Owners' Equity			
Accounts payable	$1.0 M	$\frac{\$1\,M}{\$10\,M} = 10\%$	$.10 \times \$12\,M = \$1.2\,M$
Accrued expenses	1.0 M	$\frac{\$1\,M}{\$10\,M} = 10\%$	$.10 \times \$12\,M = \$1.2\,M$
Notes payable	.5 M	NAª	no change .5 M
Long-term debt	$2.0 M	NAª	no change 2.0 M
Total liabilities	$4.5 M		$4.9 M
Common stock	$ .1 M	NAª	no change $ .1 M
Paid-in capital	.2 M	NAª	no change .2 M
Retained earnings	1.2 M		$1.2\,M + [.05 \times \$12\,M \times (1 - .5)] = 1.5\,M^b$
Common equity	$1.5 M		$1.8 M
Total	$6.0 M		Total financing provided $6.7 M
			Discretionary financing needed .5 Mᶜ
			Total $7.2 M

ªNot applicable. These account balances are assumed not to vary with sales.
ᵇProjected retained earnings equals the beginning level ($1.2 M) plus projected net income less any dividends paid. In this case net income is projected to equal 5 percent of sales, and dividends are projected to equal half of net income: $.05 \times \$12\,M \times (1 - .5) = \$300,000$
ᶜDiscretionary financing needed equals projected total assets ($7.2 M) less projected total liabilities ($4.9 M) less projected common equity ($1.8), or $7.2 M – 4.9 M – 1.8 M = $500,000.

FIGURE 4–1
Using the Percent of Sales Method to Forecast Future Financing Requirements

the firm does not have sufficient productive capacity to absorb a projected increase in sales. Thus, if sales were to rise by $1, fixed assets would rise by $.40, or 40 percent of the projected increase in sales. Note that if the fixed assets the firm currently owns were sufficient to support the projected level of new sales, these assets should not be allowed to vary with sales. If this were the case, then fixed assets would not be converted to a percent of sales and would be projected to remain unchanged for the period being forecast.

Also, we note that accounts payable and accrued expenses are the only liabilities allowed to vary with sales. Both these accounts might reasonably be expected to rise and fall with the level of firm sales; hence the use of the percent of sales forecast. Because these two categories of current liabilities normally vary directly with the level of sales, they are often referred to as **spontaneous sources of financing.** Chapter 14, which discusses working-capital management, has more to say about these forms of financing. Notes payable, long-term debt, common stock, and paid-in capital are not assumed to vary directly with the level of firm sales. These sources of financing are termed **discretionary,** in that the firm's management must make a conscious decision to seek additional financing using any one of them. Finally, we note that the level of retained earnings does vary with estimated sales. The predicted change in the level of retained earnings equals the estimated after-tax profits (projected net income) equal to 5 percent of sales or $600,000 less the common stock dividends of $300,000.

Thus, using the example from Figure 4–1, we estimate that firm sales will increase from $10 million to $12 million, which will cause the firm's needs for total assets to rise to $7.2 million. These assets will then be financed by $4.9 million in existing liabilities plus spontaneous liabilities; $1.8 million in owner funds, including $300,000 in retained earnings from next year's sales; and, finally, $500,000 in discretionary financing, which can be raised by issuing notes payable, selling bonds, offering an issue of stock, or some combination of these sources.

In summary, we can estimate the firm's needs for discretionary financing, using the percent of sales method of financial forecasting, by following a four-step procedure:

Step 1: Convert each asset and liability account that varies directly with firm sales to a percent of current year's sales.

EXAMPLE

$$\frac{\text{current assets}}{\text{sales}} = \frac{\$2\text{ M}}{\$10\text{ M}} = .2 \text{ or } 20\%$$ ■

Step 2: Project the level of each asset and liability account in the balance sheet using its percent of sales multiplied by projected sales or by leaving the account balance unchanged where the account does not vary with the level of sales.

EXAMPLE
---

projected current assets =

$$\text{projected sales} \times \frac{\text{current assets}}{\text{sales}} = \$12\text{ M} \times .2 = 2.4\text{ M}$$ ■

Step 3: Project the level of new retained earnings available to help finance the firm's operations. This equals projected net income for the period less planned common stock dividends.

EXAMPLE
---

projected addition to retained earnings =

$$\text{projected sales} \times \frac{\text{net income}}{\text{sales}} \times \left(1 - \frac{\text{cash dividends}}{\text{net income}}\right)$$

$$= \$12\text{ M} \times .05 \times [1 - .5] = \$300,000$$ ■

Step 4: Project the firm's need for discretionary financing as the projected level of total assets less projected liabilities and owners' equity.

EXAMPLE

discretionary financing needed =
projected total assets – projected total liabilities – projected owners' equity
= \$7.2 M – \$4.9 M – \$1.8 M = \$500,000   ∎

PERSPECTIVE IN FINANCE

Are you beginning to wonder exactly where finance comes into financial forecasting? To this point financial forecasting looks for all the world like financial statement forecasting. The reason is that we have adopted the accountant's model of the firm, the balance sheet, as the underlying structure of the financial forecast. The key to financial forecasting is the identification of the firm's anticipated future financing requirements, and these requirements can be identified as the "plug" figure or simply the number that balances a pro forma balance sheet.

The Discretionary Financing Needed (DFN) Model

In the preceding discussion we estimated DFN as the difference in projected total assets and the sum of projected liabilities and owner's equity. We can estimate DFN directly using the predicted change in sales (ΔS) and corresponding changes in assets, liabilities and owner's equity as follows:

$$DFN_{t+1} = \begin{matrix} \text{projected} \\ \text{change in} \\ \text{assets} \end{matrix} - \begin{matrix} \text{projected} \\ \text{change in} \\ \text{liabilities} \end{matrix} - \begin{matrix} \text{projected} \\ \text{change in} \\ \text{owner's equity} \end{matrix}$$

or   **(4–1)**

$$DFN_{t+1} = \left[\frac{assets_t^*}{sales_t} \Delta sales_{t+1} \right] - \left[\frac{liabilities_t^*}{sales_t} \Delta sales_{t+1} \right] - \left[NPM_{t+1} \cdot (1-b)\, sales_{t+1} \right]$$

where

DFN_{t+1} = predicted discretionary financing needed for period $t+1$.

$assets_t^*$ = those assets in period t that are expected to change in proportion to the level of sales. In our example we have assumed that all the firm's assets vary in proportion to sales. We will have more to say about this assumption in the next section where we consider economies of scale and lumpy fixed asset investments.

$sales_t$ = the level of sales for the period just ended.

$\Delta sales_{t+1}$ = the change in sales projected for period $t+1$, i.e., $Sales_{t+1} - Sales_t$. Note that "Δ" is the Greek symbol delta which is used here to represent "change".

liabilities$_t$* = those liabilities in period t that are expected to change in proportion to the level of sales. In our preceding example we assumed that accounts payable and accrued expenses varied with sales but notes payable and long-term debt did not.

NPM$_{t+1}$ = the net profit margin (Net Income ÷ sales) projected for period $t + 1$.

b = dividends as a percent of net income or the dividend payout ratio such that $(1 - b)$ is the proportion of the firm's projected net income that will be retained and reinvested in the firm (i.e., $(1 - b)$ is the retention ratio).

Using the numbers from the preceding example we estimate DFN$_{1994}$ as follows:

$$DFN_{1994} = \left(\frac{\$2M + 4M}{\$10M}\right)\$2M - \left(\frac{\$1M + 1M}{\$10M}\right)\$2\,M - .05 \cdot (1 - .5)\$12\,M$$

$$= \$.5 \text{ million or } \$500,000$$

Analyzing the Effects of Profitability and Dividend Policy on DFN

Using the DFN model we can quickly and easily evaluate the sensitivity of our projected financing requirements to changes in key variables. For example, using the information from the preceding example we evaluate the effect of net profit margins (NPM) ranging from 1 percent, 5 percent, and 10 percent in combination with dividend payout ratios of 30 percent, 50 percent and 70 percent as follows:

Discretionary Financing Needed
for Various Net Profit Margins and Dividend Payout Ratios

Net Profit Margin	Dividend Payout Ratios (Dividends ÷ Net Income)		
	30%	50%	70%
1%	$716,000	$740,000	$764,000
5%	380,000	500,000	620,000
10%	(40,000)	200,000	440,000

If these values for the net profit margin represent reasonable estimates of the possible ranges of values the firm might experience and if the firm is considering dividend payouts ranging from 30 percent to 70 percent, then we estimate that the firm's financing requirements (DFN) will range from ($40,000), which represents a surplus of $40,000, to a situation where it would need to acquire $764,000. Lower net profit margins mean higher funds requirements. Also, higher dividend payout percentages, other things remaining constant, lead to a need for more discretionary financing. This latter observation is a direct result of the fact that a high-dividend-paying firm retains less of its earnings.

The Sustainable Rate of Growth

The **Sustainable Rate of Growth** (g*) represents the rate at which a firm's sales can grow if it wants to maintain its present financial ratios and *does not* want to resort to the sale of new equity shares.[1] We can solve for the Sustainable Rate of Growth directly using the Discretionary Financing Needed formula found in equation 4–1 as we illustrate in the footnote found below.[2] Specifically, the Sustainable Rate of Growth is that rate of sales growth for which Discretionary Financing Needed equals zero. The resulting formula is quite simple and relies on the Return on Equity (ROE) ratio and dividend payout ratio (b).

$$\text{Sustainable Rate of Growth } (g^*) = \text{ROE } (1 - b) \qquad \textbf{(4–2)}$$

and we recall from Chapter 3 that ROE is defined as follows:

$$\text{ROE} = \frac{\text{net income}}{\text{common equity}}$$

Equation 4–2 is deceptively simple. Note that a firm's ROE is determined by a number of factors including the firm's profit margin, asset turnover and its use of financial leverage. Specifically, recall from Chapter 3 that we developed the following relationship for ROE:

$$\text{ROE} = \left(\frac{\text{net profit}}{\text{margin}} \right) \times \left(\frac{\text{total asset}}{\text{turnover}} \right) \div \left(1 - \frac{\text{debt}}{\text{ratio}} \right)$$

or

$$\text{ROE} = \left(\frac{\text{net income}}{\text{sales}} \right) \times \left(\frac{\text{sales}}{\text{assets}} \right) \div \left(\frac{\text{total debt}}{1 - \text{total assets}} \right).$$

Hence, the firm's Sustainable Rate of Growth is determined by all the determinants of its return on equity (net profit margin, total asset turnover and financial leverage) and its choice of a dividend payout ratio (b). To illustrate the calculation of the Sustainable Rate of Growth consider the financial information for the Harris Electronics Corporation found in Table 4–1.

Harris experienced reasonably stable Sustainable Rates of Growth ranging from a low of 5.80 percent in 1990 to a high of 6.40 percent in 1992. The reasons for the modest variation are easy to see from the data provided in Table 4–1. The firm's rate of return on common equity (ROCE) varied only slightly over the period, from a low of 9.67 percent

---

[1]Extensive discussion of the Sustainable Rate of Growth concept is found in Robert C. Higgins, "Sustainable Growth with Inflation," *Financial Management* (Autumn 1981): pp. 36–40.

[2]We can evaluate the impact of differing rates of sales growth on DFN by recognizing that the growth in firm sales, g, is simply the ratio of the projected change in sales (ΔSales_{t+1}) divided by the most recent past level of sales (Sales_t). Rearranging terms in equation 4–1 and substituting g for $\dfrac{\Delta\text{sales}_{t+1}}{\text{sales}_t}$ we get the following result:

$$\text{DFN}_{t+1} = g \cdot \text{assets} - \text{liabilities} \cdot g - \text{NPM} (1 - b) \text{ sales}_{t+1}$$

Note that the Sustainable Rate of Growth is that growth rate in firm sales (g^*) which makes $\text{DFN}_{t+1} = 0$. Thus, setting DFN_{t+1} in the above equation equal to zero and solving for g we get the Sustainable Rate of Growth equation:

$$\text{Sustainable Rate of Growth } (g^*) = \text{ROE}(1 - b)$$

where ROE is the return on equity (Net Income ÷ Common Equity) and b is the fraction of firm earnings paid out in dividends or the Dividend Payout Ratio.

in 1990 to a high of 11 percent in 1991, while the retention ratio (1-b) remained steady at 60 percent of earnings. Harris' actual rate of sales growth from 1990 to 1991 was 21.74% which was above its sustainable rate for 1991 which was only 5.80%. The sustainable rate of growth applicable to 1991 is calculated using data from 1990. In this year we calculated the firm's sustainable rate of growth for 1991 to be 5.80 percent [9.67%(1– .40)], but its actual increase in sales for the coming year was 21.74 percent [($1,400 – 1,150)/$1,150]. How did Harris accommodate the financing demands during 1991? The answer can be found by examining the firm's debt-to-assets ratio and changes to the firm's common equity. We see that Harris increased its borrowing from 42.56 percent of assets to 49.48 percent without issuing any new common stock. Thus, Harris has financed its DFN using new debt issues.

Limitations of the Percent of Sales Forecast Method

The **percent of sales method** of financial forecasting provides reasonable estimates of a firm's financing requirements only where asset requirements and financing sources can be accurately forecast as a constant percent of sales. For example, predicting inventories using the percent of sales method involves the following predictive equation:

$$\text{inventories}_t = \%INV \cdot \text{sales}_t$$

where %INV is the inventories-to-sales ratio.

Figure 4–2a depicts this predictive relationship. Note that the percent-of-sales predictive model is simply a straight line that passes through the origin (i.e., has a zero intercept). There are some fairly common instances in which this type of relationship fails to describe the relationship between an asset category and sales. Two such examples involve assets for which there are scale economies and assets that must be purchased in discrete quantities ("lumpy assets").

	1993	1992	1991	1990	1989
Sales	$1,500	$1,450	$1,400	$1,150	$1,090
Net Income	75	73	70	58	55
Assets	1,350	1,305	1,260	1,035	981
Dividends	30	29	28	23	21.8
Common Equity	725	680	637	595	560
Liabilities	625	625	623	440	421
Liabilities & Owner's Equity	1,350	1,305	1,260	1,035	981
Sustainable Rate of Growth (g*)	6.21%	6.40%	6.60%	5.80%	5.84%
Actual Growth Rate in Sales	NA	3.45%	3.57%	21.74%	5.50%
Return on Equity (ROCE)	10.34%	10.66%	11.00%	9.67%	9.73%
Retention Ratio (1-b)	60.00%	60.00%	60.00%	60.00%	60.00%
Debt to Assets Ratio	46.30%	47.89%	49.48%	42.56%	42.92%
New Common Stock	0	0	0	0	0

NA—Not available or cannot be calculated without 1994 data.

TABLE 4–1
Harris Electronics Corporation: Sustainable Rate of Growth Calculations

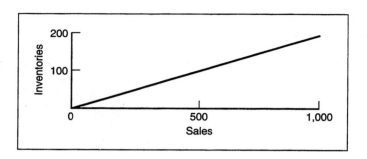

FIGURE 4–2a
Percent of Sales Forecast

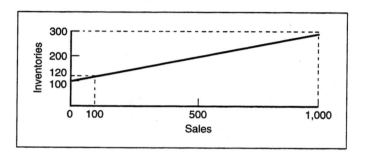

FIGURE 4–2b
Economies of Scale

Economies of scale are sometimes realized from investing in certain types of assets. This means that these assets do not increase in direct proportion to sales. Figure 4–2b reflects one instance in which the firm realizes economies of scale from its investment in inventory. Note that inventories as a percent of sales decline from 120 percent where sales are $100, to 30 percent where sales equal $1,000. This reflects the fact that there is a fixed component of inventories (in this case $100) that the firm must have on hand regardless of the level of sales, plus a variable component (20 percent of sales). In this instance the predictive equation for inventories is as follows:

$$\text{inventories}_t = a + b \text{ sales}_t$$

In this example, a is equal to 100 and b equals .20.[3]

Figure 4–2c is an example of *lumpy assets*, that is, assets that must be purchased in large, non-divisible components. Consequently, when a block of assets is purchased it creates excess capacity until sales grow to the point where the capacity is fully used. The result is a step function like the one depicted in Figure 4–2c. Thus, if the firm does not expect sales to exceed the current capacity of its plant and equipment, there would be no projected need for added plant and equipment capacity.

---

[3]Economies of scale are evidenced here by the nonzero intercept value. However, scale economies can also result in nonlinear relationships between sales and a particular asset category. Later, when we discuss cash management, we will find that one popular cash management model predicts a nonlinear relationship between the optimal cash balance and the level of cash transactions.

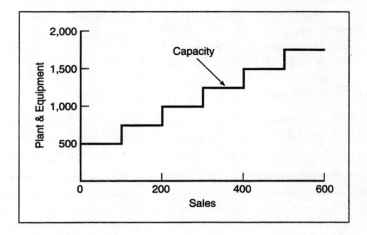

FIGURE 4–2c
Economies of Scale and
Lumpy Investments

■ FINANCIAL PLANNING AND BUDGETING

As we noted earlier, the principal virtue of the percent of sales method of financial forecasting is its simplicity. To obtain a more precise estimate of the amount and timing of the firm's future financing needs, we require a cash budget. The percent of sales method of financial forecasting provides a very useful, low-cost forerunner to the development of the more detailed cash budget, which the firm will ultimately use to estimate its financing needs.

BACK TO THE FUNDAMENTALS

Budgets have many important uses; however, their use as a tool of managerial control is critically important and often overlooked in the study of financial management. **Axiom 7: The Agency Problem—Managers Won't Work for the Owners Unless It's in Their Best Interest** speaks to the root source of the problem, and budgets provide one tool for attempting to deal with it. Specifically, budgets provide management with a tool for evaluating performance and consequently maintaining a degree of control over employee actions.

Budget Functions

A **budget** is simply a forecast of future events. For example, students preparing for final exams make use of time budgets, which help them allocate their limited preparation time among their courses. Students also must budget their financial resources among competing uses, such as books, tuition, food, rent, clothes, and extracurricular activities.

Budgets perform three basic functions for a firm. First, they indicate the amount and timing of the firm's needs for future financing. Second, they provide the basis for taking corrective action in the event budgeted figures do not match actual or realized figures. Third, budgets provide the basis for performance evaluation. Plans are carried out by people, and budgets provide benchmarks that management can use to evaluate the performance of those responsible for carrying out those plans and, in turn, to control their actions. Thus, budgets are valuable aids in both the planning and controlling aspects of the firm's financial management.

The Cash Budget

The **cash budget** represents a detailed plan of future cash flows and is composed of four elements: cash receipts, cash disbursements, net change in cash for the period, and new financing needed.

EXAMPLE

To demonstrate the construction and use of the cash budget, consider Salco Furniture Company, Inc., a regional distributor of household furniture. Management is in the process of preparing a monthly cash budget for the upcoming six-months (January through June 1994). Salco's sales are highly seasonal, peaking in the months of March through May. Roughly 30 percent of Salco's sales are collected one month after the sale, 50 percent two months after the sale, and the remainder during the third month following the sale.

Salco attempts to pace its purchases with its forecast of future sales. Purchases generally equal 75 percent of sales and are made two months in advance of anticipated sales. Payments are made in the month following purchases. For example, June sales are estimated at $100,000, thus April purchases are .75 × $100,000 = $75,000. Correspondingly, payments for purchases in May equal $75,000. Wages, salaries, rent, and other cash expenses are recorded in Table 4–2, which gives Salco's cash budget for the six-month period ended in June 1994. Additional expenditures are recorded in the cash budget related to the purchase of equipment in the amount of $14,000 during February and the repayment of a $12,000 loan in May. In June Salco will pay $7,500 interest on its $150,000 in long-term debt for the period of January-June 1994. Interest on the $12,000 short-term note repaid in May for the period January through May equals $600 and is paid in May.

Salco currently has a cash balance of $20,000 and wants to maintain a minimum balance of $10,000. Additional borrowing necessary to maintain that minimum balance is estimated in the final section of Table 4–2. Borrowing takes place at the beginning of the month in which the funds are needed. Interest on borrowed funds equals 12 percent per annum, or 1 percent per month, and is paid in the month following the one in which funds are borrowed. Thus, interest on funds borrowed in January will be paid in February equal to 1 percent of the loan amount outstanding during January.

The financing-needed line on Salco's cash budget indicates that the firm's cumulative short-term borrowing will be $36,350 in February, $65,874 in March, $86,633 in April, and $97,599 in May. In June the firm will be able to reduce its borrowing to $79,875. Note that the cash budget indicates not only the amount of financing needed during the period but also when the funds will be needed. ■

Fixed Versus Flexible Budgets

The cash budget given in Table 4–2 for Salco, Inc. is an example of a **fixed budget.** Cash flow estimates are made for a single set of monthly sales estimates. Thus, the estimates of expenses and new financing needed are meaningful only for the level of sales for which they were computed. To avoid this limitation, several budgets corresponding to different sets of sales estimates can be prepared. Such a **flexible budget** fulfills two basic needs: First, it gives information regarding the range of the firm's possible financing needs, and second, it provides a standard against which to measure the performance of subordinates who are responsible for the various cost and revenue items contained in the budget.

This second function deserves some additional comment. The obvious problem that arises relates to the fact that costs vary with the actual level of sales experienced by the firm. Thus, if the budget is to be used as a standard for performance evaluation or control, it must be constructed to match realized sales and production figures. This can involve much more than simply "adjusting cost figures up or down in proportion to the deviation of actual from planned sales"; that is, costs may not vary in strict proportion to sales, just as inventory levels may not vary as a constant percent of sales. Thus, preparation of a flexible budget involves re-estimating all the cash expenses that would be incurred at each of several possible sales levels. This process might utilize a variant of the percent of sales method discussed earlier.

Budget Period

There are no strict rules for determining the length of the budget period. However, as a general rule it should be long enough to show the effect of management policies yet short enough so that estimates can be made

Worksheet	Oct.	Nov.	Dec.
Sales	$55,000	$62,000	$50,000
Collections:			
First month (30%)			
Second month (50%)			
Third month (20%)			
Total			
Purchases (75% of sales in two months)			$56,250
Payments (one-month lag)			
Cash receipts:			
Collections			
Cash disbursements:			
Purchases			
Wages and salaries			
Rent			
Other expenses			
Interest expense on existing debt			
($12,000 note and $150,000 in long-term debt)			
Taxes			
Purchase of equipment			
Loan repayment ($12,000 note due in May)			
Total disbursements:			
Net monthly charge			
Plus: Beginning cash balance			
Less: Interest on short-term borrowing			
Equals: Ending cash balance before short-term no borrowing			
Financing needed[a]			
Ending cash balance			
Cumulative borrowing			

[a]The amount of financing that is required to raise the firm's ending cash balance up to its $10,000 desired cash balance.

with reasonable accuracy. Applying this rule of thumb to the Salco example in Table 4–2, it appears that the six-month budget period is too short. The reason is that we cannot tell whether the planned operations of the firm will be successful over the coming fiscal year. That is, for most of the first six-month period the firm is operating with a cash flow deficit. If this does not reverse in the latter six months of the year, then a reevaluation of the firm's plans and policies is clearly in order.

Longer-range budgets are also prepared in the form of the **capital-expenditure budget.** This budget details the firm's plans for acquiring plant and equipment over a 5-year, 10-year, or even longer period. Furthermore, firms often develop comprehensive long-range plans extending up to 10 years into the future. These plans are generally not as detailed as the annual cash budget, but they do consider such major components as sales, capital expenditures, new-product development, capital funds acquisition, and employment needs.

Jan.	Feb.	Mar.	Apr.	May	June	July	Aug.
$60,000	$75,000	$88,000	$100,000	$110,000	$100,000	$80,000	$75,000
15,000	18,000	22,500	26,400	30,000	33,000		
31,000	25,000	30,000	37,500	44,000	50,000		
11,000	12,400	10,000	12,000	15,000	17,600		
$57,000	55,400	62,500	75,900	89,000	100,600		
66,000	75,000	82,500	75,000	60,000	56,250		
56,250	66,000	75,000	82,500	75,000	60,000		
$57,000	55,400	62,500	75,900	89,000	100,600		
$56,250	66,000	75,000	82,500	75,000	60,000		
3,000	10,000	7,000	8,000	6,000	4,000		
4,000	4,000	4,000	4,000	4,000	4,000		
1,000	500	1,200	1,500	1,500	1,200		
				600	7,500		
		4,460			5,200		
	14,000						
				12,000			
$64,250	94,500	91,660	96,000	99,100	81,900		
$(7,250)	(39,100)	(29,160)	(20,100)	(10,100)	18,700		
20,000	12,750	10,000	10,000	10,000	10,000		
—	—	(364)	(659)	(866)	(976)		
12,750	(26,350)	(19,524)	(10,759)	(966)	27,724		
—	36,350	29,524	20,759	10,966	(17,724)[b]		
$12,750	10,000	10,,000	10,000	10,000	10,000		
—	36,350	65,874	86,633	97,599	79,875		

[b]Negative financing needed simply means the firm has excess cash that can be used to retire a part of its short-term borrowing from prior months.

■ COMPUTERIZED FINANCIAL PLANNING

In recent years a number of developments in both computer hardware (machines) and software (programs) have reduced the tedium of the planning and budgeting process immensely. These include the introduction of "user-friendly" or "easy-to-use" computer programs that are specialized for application to financial planning.

Financial planning software packages (sometimes referred to as electronic spreadsheets) were first made popular on large mainframe computers but quickly spread to personal computers in the early eighties. These packages allow even a computer novice to use a personal computer to construct budgets and forecasts. The real advantage of the computer is realized when there is a need for different scenarios to be evaluated quickly and easily.

FINANCIAL MANAGEMENT IN PRACTICE

Management's Ability to Forecast Accurately

In spite of the importance of forecasting to strategic planning, managers have mixed success in forecasting events and outcomes accurately.* Inaccuracies, when they occur, have more to do with the nature of the environment than with management effort.

There is no shortage of dramatic examples to illustrate carefully designed forecasts that were widely off the mark. In the 1970s school administrators closed elementary schools as enrollments dropped. Forecasting that women's liberation had permanently reduced the birthrate, administrators acted to close schools permanently and, in some cases, even sell them. What happened, however, was that women merely delayed their childbearing years. In the mid-1980s, many of these same administrators found enrollments back at near-record levels.

As another example, the three most important economic outcomes of the Reagan era (1981–88) have been characterized as a high structural fiscal deficit, a chronic balance of payments deficit, and high real interest rates. Yet not one of these was predicted in 1979–80. Finally, most experts thought that the October 1987 stock market crash would bring on a recession in 1988. Managers who strategically positioned their organizations for the 1988 recession found that it didn't come.

Forecasting techniques are most accurate when the environment is static. The more dynamic the environment, the more likely management is to develop inaccurate forecasts. Forecasting has a relatively unimpressive record in predicting nonseasonal turning points such as recessions, unusual events, discontinuities, and the actions or reactions of competitors. The only major consolation for managers is that their competitors are unlikely to be any better than they are at forecasting accurately in a dynamic environment.

Although forecasting has a mixed record, managers continue to engage in the practice. They find that for many factors—such as revenues, demographic trends, new laws, and labor supplies—forecasting's record is quite solid. Moreover, by shortening the length of forecasts, managers improve their accuracy.

---

*This section is based on Essam Mahmoud, "Accuracy in Forecasting: A Survey," *Journal of Forecasting* 3: (1984), 139–59; Reed Moyer, "The Futility of Forecasting," *Long-Range Planning* (February 1983), 65–72; and Ronald Bailey, "Them That Can, Do; Them That Can't, Forecast," *Forbes* (December 26, 1988), 94–100. Used by Permission from Stephen P. Robbins, *Management*, 3d ed., p. 253. © 1991 Prentice Hall Publishing Co.

Another major development that has had a significant impact on the extent to which computers are used in the planning and budgeting process is the advent of the personal computer. For mere hundreds of dollars the financial analyst's desk can contain the computing power it took hundreds of thousands of dollars to buy just a decade ago. The development of financial planning software has paralleled the development of microcomputer technology. The number of spreadsheet packages has mushroomed over the past five years. These packages generally sell for less than $500 and include graphics programs as well as elementary database management capabilities.[4]

---

[4]The number and variety of financial spreadsheet programs has expanded dramatically since the introduction of the original Visi-Calc program. These include Lotus 1-2-3 and Excel, among others. In addition, there is a growing set of products referred to as "expert systems," which attempt to mimic the decisions of experts. To date these efforts have produced a limited number of financial applications software related to such things as the capital budgeting decision, but they offer an opportunity to expand the capabilities of the financial manager of the future.

SUMMARY

This chapter develops the role of forecasting within the context of the firm's financial planning efforts. Forecasts of the firm's sales revenues and related expenses provide the basis for projecting future financing needs. The most popular method for forecasting financial variables is the percent of sales method.

Forecasts of firm sales and expenses are used to develop the cash budget for the planning period, which is then used to estimate the firm's future financing needs. In this chapter all needed financing is supplied through short-term notes. However, in Chapters 12 and 14 we will look more closely at sources of financing. Chapter 12 addresses the choice among long-term sources (bonds, preferred stock, and common stock) while Chapter 14 deals with the choice between current (short-term) financing versus long-term financing.

STUDY QUESTIONS

4–1. Discuss the shortcomings of the percent-of-sales method of financial forecasting.

4–2. Explain how a fixed cash budget differs from a variable or flexible cash budget.

4–3. What two basic needs does a flexible (variable) cash budget serve?

4–4. What would be the probable effect on a firm's cash position of the following events?
 a. Rapidly rising sales
 b. A delay in the payment of payables
 c. A more liberal credit policy on sales (to the firm's customers)
 d. Holding larger inventories

4–5. How long should the budget period be? Why would a firm not set a rule that all budgets be for a 12-month period?

4–6. A cash budget is usually thought of as a means of planning for future financing needs. Why would a cash budget also be important for a firm that had excess cash on hand?

4–7. Explain why a cash budget would be of particular importance to a firm that experiences seasonal fluctuations in its sales.

SELF-TEST PROBLEMS

ST-1. *(Financial Forecasting)* Use the percent of sales method to prepare a pro forma income statement for Calico Sales Co., Inc. Projected sales for next year equal $4 million. Cost of goods sold equals 70 percent of sales, administrative expense equals $500,000, and depreciation expense is $300,000. Interest expense equals $50,000 and income is taxed at a rate of 40 percent. The firm plans to spend $200,000 during the period to renovate its office facility and will retire $150,000 in notes payable. Finally, selling expense equals 5 percent of sales.

ST-2. *(Cash Budget)* Stauffer, Inc., has estimated sales and purchase requirements for the last half of the coming year. Past experience indicates that it will collect 20 percent of its sales in the month of the sale, 50 percent of the remainder one month after the sale, and the balance in the second month following the sale. Stauffer prefers to pay for half its purchases in the month of the purchase and the other half the following month. Labor expense for each month is expected to equal 5 percent of that month's sales, with cash payment being made in the month in which the expense is incurred. Depreciation expense is $5,000 per month; miscellaneous cash expenses are $4,000 per month and are paid in the month incurred. General and administrative expenses of $50,000 are recognized and paid monthly. A $60,000 truck is to be purchased in August and is to be depreciated on a straight-line basis over 10 years with no expected salvage value. The company also plans to pay a $9,000 cash dividend to stockholders in July. The company feels that a minimum cash balance of $30,000 should be maintained. Any borrowing will cost 12 percent annually, with interest paid in the month following the month in which the funds are borrowed. Borrowing takes place at the beginning of the month in which the need for funds arises. For example, if during the month of July the firm should need to borrow $24,000 to maintain its $30,000 desired minimum balance, then $24,000 will be taken out on July 1 with interest owed for the entire month of July. Interest for the month of July would then be paid on August 1. Sales and purchase estimates are shown below. Prepare a cash budget for the months of July and August (cash on hand June 30 was $30,000, while sales for May and June were $100,000 and purchases were $60,000 for each of these months).

Month	Sales	Purchases
July	$120,000	$50,000
August	150,000	40,000
September	110,000	30,000

STUDY PROBLEMS

4–1. *(Financial Forecasting)* Sambonoza Enterprises projects its sales next year to be $4 million and expects to earn 5 percent of that amount after taxes. The firm is currently in the process of projecting its financing needs and has made the following assumptions (projections):
  1. Current assets will equal 20 percent of sales while fixed assets will remain at their current level of $1 million.
  2. Common equity is currently $0.8 million, and the firm pays out half its after-tax earnings in dividends.
  3. The firm has short-term payables and trade credit that normally equal 10 percent of sales and has no long-term debt outstanding.
  What are Sambonoza's financing needs for the coming year?

4–2. *(Financial Forecasting—Percent of Sales)* Tulley Appliances, Inc., projects next year's sales to be $20 million. Current sales are at $15 million based on current assets of $5 million and fixed assets of $5 million. The firm's net profit margin is 5 percent after taxes. Tulley forecasts that current assets will rise in direct proportion to the increase in sales, but fixed assets will increase by only $100,000. Currently, Tulley has $1.5 million in accounts payable plus $2 million in long-term debt (due in 10 years) outstanding and common equity (including $4 million in retained earnings) totaling $6.5 million. Tulley plans to pay $500,000 in common stock dividends next year.

a. What are Tulley's total financing needs (i.e., total assets) for the coming year?

b. Given the firm's projections and dividend payment plans, what are its discretionary financing needs?

c. Based on the projections given and assuming that the $100,000 expansion in fixed assets will occur, what is the largest increase in sales the firm can support without having to resort to the use of discretionary sources of financing?

4–3. *(Pro Forma Balance Sheet Construction)* Use the following industry average ratios to construct a pro forma balance sheet for Carlos Menza Inc.

Total asset turnover	2 times
Average collection period (assume a 365-day year)	9 days
Fixed asset turnover	5 times
Inventory turnover (based on cost of goods sold)	3 times
Current ratio	2 times
Sales (all on credit)	$4.0 million
Cost of goods sold	75% of sales
Debt ratio	50%

Cash		Current liabilities	
Accounts receivable		Long-term debt	
		Common stock plus	
Net fixed assets		retained earnings	
	$ _____		$ _____

4–4. *(Cash Budget)* The Sharpe Corporation's projected sales for the first eight months of 1993 are as follows:

January	$90,000	May	$300,000
February	120,000	June	270,000
March	135,000	July	225,000
April	240,000	August	150,000

Of Sharpe's sales, 10 percent is for cash, another 60 percent is collected in the month following sale, and 30 percent is collected in the second month following sale. November and December sales for 1992 were $220,000 and $175,000, respectively.

Sharpe purchases its raw materials two months in advance of its sales equal to 60 percent of their final sales price. The supplier is paid one month after it makes delivery. For example, purchases for April sales are made in February and payment is made in March.

In addition, Sharpe pays $10,000 per month for rent and $20,000 each month for other expenditures. Tax prepayments of $22,500 are made each quarter, beginning in March.

The company's cash balance at December 31, 1992, was $22,000; a minimum balance of $15,000 must be maintained at all times. Assume that any short-term financing needed to maintain the cash balance would be paid off in the month following the month of financing if sufficient funds are available. Interest on short-term loans (12 percent) is paid monthly. Borrowing to meet estimated monthly cash needs takes place at the beginning of the month. Thus, if in the month of April the firm expects to have a need for an additional $60,500, these funds would be borrowed at the beginning of April with interest of $605 ($.12 \times 1/12 \times \$60,500$) owed for April and paid at the beginning of May.

   a. Prepare a cash budget for Sharpe covering the first seven months of 1993.

   b. Sharpe has $200,000 in notes payable due in July that must be repaid or renegotiated for an extension. Will the firm have ample cash to repay the notes?

4–5. *(Percent-of-Sales Forecasting)* Which of the following accounts would most likely vary directly with the level of firm sales? Discuss each briefly.

	Yes	No
Cash	____	____
Marketable securities	____	____
Accounts payable	____	____
Notes payable	____	____
Plant and equipment	____	____
Inventories	____	____

4–6. *(Financial Forecasting—Percent of Sales)* The balance sheet of the Thompson Trucking Company (TTC) follows:

Thompson Trucking Company Balance Sheet, December 31, 1993 ($ millions)

Current assets	$10	Accounts payable	$5
Net fixed assets	15	Notes payable	0
Total	$25	Bonds payable	10
		Common equity	10
		Total	$25

TTC had sales for the year ended 12/31/93 of $50 million. The firm follows a policy of paying all net earnings out to its common stockholders in cash dividends. Thus, TTC generates no funds from its earnings that can be used to expand its operations. (Assume that depreciation expense is just equal to the cost of replacing worn-out assets.)

   a. If TTC anticipates sales of $80 million during the coming year, develop a pro forma balance sheet for the firm for 12/31/94. Assume that current assets vary as a percent of sales, net fixed assets remain unchanged, accounts payable vary as a percent of sales, and use notes payable as a balancing entry.

   b. How much "new" financing will TTC need next year?

   c. What limitations does the percent of sales forecast method suffer from? Discuss briefly.

4–7. *(Financial Forecasting—Discretionary Financing Needed)* The most recent balance sheet for the Armadillo Dog Biscuit Co. is shown in the table below. The company is about to embark on an advertising campaign, which is expected to raise sales from the current level of $5 million to $7 million by the end of next year. The firm is currently operating at full capacity and will have to increase its investment in both current and fixed assets to support the projected level of new sales. In fact, the firm estimates that both categories of assets will rise in direct proportion to the projected increase in sales.

The firm's net profits were 6 percent of current year's sales but are expected to rise to 7 percent of next year's sales. To help support its anticipated growth in asset needs next year, the firm has suspended plans to pay cash dividends to its stockholders. In past years a $1.50 per share dividend has been paid annually.

Armadillo Dog Biscuit Co., Inc. ($ millions)

	Present Level	Percent of Sales	Projected Level
Current assets	$2.0		
Net fixed assets	3.0		
Total	$5.0		
Accounts payable	$0.5		
Accrued expenses	0.5		
Notes payable	—		
Current liabilities	$1.0		
Long-term debt	$2.0		
Common stock	0.5		
Retained earnings	1.5		
Common equity	$2.0		
Total	$5.0		

Armadillo's payables and accrued expenses are expected to vary directly with sales. In addition, notes payable will be used to supply the funds that are needed to finance next year's operations and that are not forthcoming from other sources.

a. Fill in the table and project the firm's needs for discretionary financing. Use notes payable as the balancing entry for future discretionary financing needed.

b. Compare Armadillo's current ratio and debt ratio (total liabilities/total assets) before the growth in sales and after. What was the effect of the expanded sales on these two dimensions of Armadillo's financial condition?

c. What difference, if any, would have resulted if Armadillo's sales had risen to $6 million in one year and $7 million only after two years? Discuss only; no calculations required.

4-8. (Forecasting Discretionary Financing Needs) Fishing Charter, Inc., estimates that it invests 30 cents in assets for each dollar of new sales. However, 5 cents in profits are produced by each dollar of additional sales, of which 1 cent can be reinvested in the firm. If sales rise from their current level of $5 million by $500,000 next year, and the ratio of spontaneous liabilities to sales is .15, what will be the firm's need for discretionary financing? (Hint: In this situation you do not know what the firm's existing level of assets is, nor do you know how those assets have been financed. Thus, you must estimate the change in financing needs and match this change with the expected changes in spontaneous liabilities, retained earnings, and other sources of discretionary financing.)

4–9. *(Preparation of a Cash Budget)* Harrison Printing has projected its sales for the first eight months of 1993 as follows:

January	$100,000	May	$275,000
February	120,000	June	200,000
March	150,000	July	200,000
April	300,000	August	180,000

Harrison collects 20 percent of its sales in the month of the sale, 50 percent in the month following the sale, and the remaining 30 percent two months following the sale. During November and December of 1992 Harrison's sales were $220,000 and $175,000, respectively.

Harrison purchases raw materials two months in advance of its sales equal to 65 percent of its final sales. The supplier is paid one month after delivery. Thus, purchases for April sales are made in February and payment is made in March.

In addition, Harrison pays $10,000 per month for rent and $20,000 each month for other expenditures. Tax prepayments of $22,500 are made each quarter beginning in March. The company's cash balance as of December 31, 1992, was $22,000; a minimum balance of $20,000 must be maintained at all times to satisfy the firm's bank line of credit agreement. Harrison has arranged with its bank for short-term credit at an interest rate of 12 percent per annum (1 percent per month) to be paid monthly. Borrowing to meet estimated monthly cash needs takes place at the end of the month, and interest is not paid until the end of the following month. Consequently, if the firm were to need to borrow $50,000 during the month of April, then it would pay $500 (= .01 × $50,000) in interest during May. Finally, Harrison follows a policy of repaying any outstanding short-term debt in any month in which its cash balance exceeds the minimum desired balance of $20,000.

a. Harrison needs to know what its cash requirements will be for the next six months so that it can renegotiate the terms of its short-term credit agreement with its bank, if necessary. To evaluate this problem the firm plans to evaluate the impact of a ± 20 percent variation in its monthly sales efforts. Prepare a six-month cash budget for Harrison and use it to evaluate the firm's cash needs.

b. Harrison has a $200,000 note due in June. Will the firm have sufficient cash to repay the loan?

4–10. *(Sustainable Rate of Growth)* ADP, Inc., is a manufacturer of specialty circuit boards used in the personal computer industry. The firm has experienced phenomenal sales growth over its short five-year life. Selected financial statement data are found in the following table:

	19x5	19x4	19x3	19x2	19x1
Sales	$3,000	$2,200	$1,800	$1,400	$1,200
Net Income	150	110	90	70	60
Assets	2,700	1,980	1,620	1,260	1,080
Dividends	60	44	36	28	24
Common Equity	812	722	656	602	560
Liabilities	1,888	1,258	964	658	520
Liabilities & Equity	2,700	1,980	1,620	1,260	1,080

    a. Calculate ADP's Sustainable Rate of Growth for each of the five years of its existence.

    b. Compare the actual rates of growth in sales to the firm's sustainable rates calculated in part a. How has ADP been financing its growing asset needs?

4–11. *(Sustainable Rate of Growth)* The Carrera Game Company has experienced a 100% increase in sales over the last five years. The company president, Jack Cerrera, has become increasingly alarmed by the firm's rising debt level even in the face of continued profitability.

	19x7	19x6	19x5	19x4	19x3
Sales	$60,000	$56,000	$48,000	$36,000	$30,000
Net Income	3,000	2,800	2,400	1,800	1,500
Assets	54,000	50,400	43,200	32,400	27,000
Dividends	1200	1,120	960	720	600
Common Equity	21,000	19,200	17,520	16,080	15,000
Liabilities	33,000	31,200	25,680	16,320	12,000
Liabilities and Equity	54,000	50,400	43,200	32,400	27,000

    a. Calculate the debt to assets ratio, return on common equity, actual rate of growth in firm sales and retention ratio for each of the five years of data provided above.

    b. Calculate the Sustainable Rates of Growth for Carrera for each of the last five years. Why has the firm's borrowing increased so dramatically?

4–12. *(Forecasting Inventories)* Findlay Instruments produces a complete line of medical instruments used by plastic surgeons and has experienced rapid growth over the last five years. In an effort to make more accurate predictions of its financing requirements Findlay is currently attempting to construct a financial planning model based on the percent of sales forecasting method. However, the firm's chief financial analyst (Sarah Macias) is concerned that the projections for inventories will be seriously in error. She recognizes that the firm has begun to accrue substantial economies of scale in its inventory investment and has documented this fact in the following data and calculations:

Year	Sales (000)	Inventory (000)	% of Sales
19X1	$15,000	1,150	7.67%
19X2	18,000	1,180	6.56%
19X3	17,500	1,175	6.71%
19X4	20,000	1,200	6.00%
19X5	25,000	1,250	5.00%
		Average	6.39%

a. Plot Findlay's sales and inventories for the last five years. What is the relationship between these two variables?

b. Estimate firm inventories for 19X6 where firm sales are projected to reach $30,000,000. Use the average percent of sales for the last five years, the most recent percent of sales and your evaluation of the true relationship between the sales and inventories from part a to make three predications.

SELF-TEST SOLUTIONS

SS-1.

Calico Sales Co., Inc., Pro Forma Income Statement

Sales		$4,000,000
Cost of goods sold (70%)		(2,800,000)
Gross profit		1,200,000
Operating expense		
Selling expense (5%)	$200,000	
Administrative expense	500,000	
Depreciation expense	300,000	(1,000,000)
Net operating income		200,000
Interest		(50,000)
Earnings before taxes		150,000
Taxes (40%)		(60,000)
Net income		$ 90,000

Although the office renovation expenditure and debt retirement are surely cash outflows, they do not enter the income statement directly. These expenditures affect expenses for the period's income statement only through their effect on depreciation and interest expense. A cash budget would indicate the full cash impact of the renovation and debt retirement expenditures.

	May	June	July	Aug.
Sales	$100,000	$100,000	$120,000	$150,000
Purchases	60,000	60,000	50,000	40,000

Cash Receipts:

	May	June	July	Aug.
Collections from month of sale (20%)	20,000	20,000	24,000	30,000
1 month later (50% of uncollected amount)		40,000	48,000	48,000
2 months later (balance)			40,000	40,000
Total receipts			$104,000	$118,000

Cash Disbursements:

	May	June	July	Aug.
Payments for purchases—				
From 1 month earlier			$30,000	$25,000
From current month			$25,000	20,000
Total			$55,000	$45,000
Miscellaneous cash expenses			4,000	4,000
Labor expense (5% of sales)			6,000	7,500
General and administrative expense ($50,000 per month)			50,000	50,000
Truch purchase			0	60,000
Cash dividends			9,000	—
Total disbursements			$(124,000)	$(166,500)

	May	June	July	Aug.
Net change in cash			(20,000)	(48,500)
Plus: Beginning cash balance			30,000	30,000
Less: Interest on short-term borrowing (1% of prior month's borrowing)				(200)
Equals: Ending cash balance—without borrowing			10,000	(18,700)
Financing needed to reach target cash balance			20,000	48,700
Cumulative borrowing			$ 20,000	$ 68,700

CHAPTER 9
CAPITAL-BUDGETING TECHNIQUES AND PRACTICE

Finding Profitable Projects • Capital-Budgeting Decision Criteria
• Capital Rationing • Ethics in Capital Budgeting • A Glance at Actual
Capital-Budgeting Practices

In Chapter 5 we developed tools for comparing cash flows that occur in different periods. This chapter uses these techniques in conjunction with additional decision rules to determine when to invest money in long-term assets, a process called **capital budgeting.** In evaluating capital investment proposals, we compare the costs and benefits of each in a number of ways. Some of these methods take into account the time value of money, others do not; however, each of these methods is used frequently in the real world. As you will see, our preferred method of analysis will be the net present value (NPV) method that compares the present value of inflows and outflows.

Capital budgeting is a decision-making process for investment in fixed assets; specifically, it involves measuring the incremental cash flows associated with investment proposals and evaluating the attractiveness of these cash flows relative to the project's cost. Typically these investments involve rather large cash outlays at the outset and commit the firm to a particular course of action over a relatively long period. Thus, if a capital-budgeting decision is incorrect, reversing it tends to be costly.

INTRODUCTION VIDEO CASE 3

Investing in Employee Productivity: An
Application of Capital Budgeting
from ABC News, Business World, October 14, 1990

This chapter and chapter 10 focus on methods used to evaluate the investment opportunities available to the firm. The capital-budgeting problems included in most financial management texts typically involve analyses of investments in new product lines or the process of replacing an old machine with a new, more efficient machine. It is fairly clear how one might estimate the sales of the new products, the savings from more efficient production, and the costs of acquiring the new machines. However, many situations faced by managers are not so straightforward. In this video case we examine a slightly different type of investment—investing in employee morale and commitment. The managers of Fel-Pro, a small manufacturer of gaskets in the Midwest, have decided that making investments in employee morale is good business. Employees receive cash bonuses on special occasions such as marriage, graduation, and birthdays; the firm provides day care for employee's children, a vacation ranch, and profit sharing.
While investing in employee productivity what does the firm expect as a return, how should costs and benefits be measured, should the NPV technique be applied, and is such an investment appropriate?

For example, about 35 years ago the Ford Motor Company's decision to produce the Edsel entailed an outlay of $250 million to bring the car to market and losses of approximately $200 million during the 2½ years it was produced—in all, a $450 million mistake.[1] This type of decision is costly to reverse. Fortunately for Ford, it was able to convert Edsel production facilities to produce the Mustang, thereby avoiding an even larger loss. In the 1980s General Motors made a major capital-budgeting decision by investing $3.5 billion to construct its Saturn automobile plant. As of 1993 sales looked good, but only time will tell if this decision proves to be profitable in the long run.

In this chapter we look first at the difficulties associated with finding profitable projects. Four capital-budgeting criteria are subsequently provided for evaluating capital investments, followed by a discussion of the problems created when the number of projects that can be accepted or the total budget is limited. Chapter 9 closes with an examination of capital budgeting in practice.

■ FINDING PROFITABLE PROJECTS

Without question it is easier to evaluate profitable projects than it is to find them. In competitive markets, generating ideas for profitable projects is extremely difficult. The competition is brisk for new profitable projects, and once they have been uncovered competitors generally rush

---
[1]"The Edsel Dies, and Ford Regroups Survivors," *Business Week,* November 28, 1959, p. 27.

in, pushing down prices and profits. For this reason a firm must have a systematic strategy for generating capital-budgeting projects. Without this flow of new projects and ideas, the firm cannot grow or even survive for long, being forced to live off the profits from existing projects with limited lives. So where do these ideas come from for new products, for ways to improve existing products, or for ways to make existing products more profitable? The answer is from inside the firm — from everywhere inside the firm.

BACK TO THE FUNDAMENTALS

The fact that profitable projects are difficult to find relates directly to **Axiom 5: The Curse of Competitive Markets—Why It's Hard to Find Exceptionally Profitable Projects.** When we introduced that axiom we stated that successful investments involve the reduction of competition by creating barriers to entry either through product differentiation or cost advantages. The key to locating profitable projects is to understand how and where they exist.

Typically a firm has a research and development department that searches for ways of improving on existing products or finding new products. These ideas may come from within the R&D department or be based on referral ideas from executives, sales personnel, or anyone in the firm. For example, at Ford Motor Company prior to the 1980s, ideas for product improvement had typically been generated in Ford's research and development department. Unfortunately, this strategy was not enough to keep Ford from losing much of its market share to the Japanese. In an attempt to cut costs and improve product quality, Ford moved from strict reliance on an R&D department to seeking the input of employees at all levels for new ideas. Bonuses are now provided to workers for their cost-cutting suggestions, and assembly line personnel who can see the production process from a hands-on point of view are now brought into the hunt for new projects. The effect on Ford has been positive and significant. Although not all suggested projects prove to be profitable, many new ideas generated from within the firm turn out to be good ones. The best way to evaluate new investment proposals is the topic of the remainder of this chapter.

◼ CAPITAL-BUDGETING DECISION CRITERIA

In deciding whether to accept a new project we will focus on the cash flows. Cash flows represent the benefits generated from accepting a capital-budgeting proposal. In this chapter we will assume a given cash flow is generated by a project and work on determining whether that project should be accepted.

We will consider four commonly used criteria for determining acceptability of investment proposals. The first one is the least sophisticated, in that it does not incorporate the time value of money into its calculations; the other three do take it into account. For the time being, the problem of incorporating risk into the capital-budgeting decision is ignored. This issue will be examined in Chapter 10. In addition, we will assume that the appropriate discount rate, required rate of return, or cost of capital is given. The determination of this rate is the topic of Chapter 11.

Payback Period

The **payback period** is the number of years needed to recover the initial cash outlay. As this criterion measures how quickly the project will return its original investment, it deals with cash flows rather than accounting profits. It also ignores the time value of money and does not discount these cash flows back to the present. The accept-reject criterion involves whether the project's payback period is less than or equal to the firm's maximum desired payback period. For example, if a firm's maximum desired payback period is three years and an investment proposal requires an initial cash outlay of $10,000 and yields the following set of annual cash flows, what is its payback period? Should the project be accepted?

Year	After Tax Cash Flow
1	$2,000
2	4,000
3	3,000
4	3,000
5	1,000

In this case, after three years the firm will have recaptured $9,000 on an initial investment of $10,000, leaving $1,000 of the initial investment to be recouped. During the fourth year a total of $3,000 will be returned from this investment, and, assuming it will flow into the firm at a constant rate over the year, it will take one-third of the year ($1,000/$3,000) to recapture the remaining $1,000. Thus, the payback period on this project is three and a third years, which is more than the desired payback period. Using the payback period criterion, the firm would reject this project.

Although the payback period is used frequently, it does have some rather obvious drawbacks, which can best be demonstrated through the use of an example. Consider two investment projects, A and B, which involve an initial cash outlay of $10,000 each and produce the annual cash flows shown in Table 9–1. Both projects have a payback period of two years; therefore, in terms of the payback period criterion both are equally acceptable. However, if we had our choice, it is clear we would select A over B, for at least two reasons. First, regardless of what happens after the payback period, project A returns our initial investment to us earlier within the payback period. Thus, if there is a time value of money, the cash flows occurring within the payback period should not be weighted equally, as they are. In addition, all cash flows that occur after the payback period are ignored. This violates the principle that investors desire more in the way of benefits rather than less—a principle that is difficult to deny, especially when we are talking about money.

	Projects	
	A	B
Initial cash outlay	–$10,000	–$10,000
Annual net cash inflows:		
Year 1	$ 6,000	$ 5,000
2	4,000	5,000
3	3,000	0
4	2,000	0
5	1,000	0

TABLE 9–1
Payback Period Example

To deal with the criticism that the payback period ignores the time value of money, some firms use the **discounted payback period** approach. The discounted payback period method is similar to the traditional payback period except that it uses discounted net cash flows rather than actual undiscounted net cash flows in calculating the payback period. The discounted payback period is defined as the number of years needed to recover the initial cash outlay from the **discounted net cash flows.** The accept-reject criterion then becomes whether the project's discounted payback period is less than or equal to the firm's maximum desired discounted payback period. Using the assumption that the required rate of return on projects A and B illustrated in Table 9–1 is 17 percent, the discounted cash flows from these projects are given in Table 9–2. The discounted payback period for Project A is 3.07 years, calculated as follows:

$$\text{Discounted Payback Period}_A = 3.0 + \$74/\$1,068 = 3.07 \text{ years.}$$

If Project A's discounted payback period was less than the firm's maximum desired discounted payback period, then Project A would be accepted. Project B, on the other hand, does not have a discounted payback period because it never fully recovers the project's initial cash outlay, and thus should be rejected. The major problem with the discounted payback period comes in setting the firm's maximum desired discounted payback period. This is an arbitrary decision that affects which projects are accepted and which ones are rejected. Thus, while the discounted payback period is superior to the traditional payback period, in that it accounts for the time value of money in its calculations, its use is limited

TABLE 9–2
Discounted Payback Period
Example Using a 17 Percent
Required Rate of Return

Project A

Year	Undiscounted Cash Flows	$PVIF_{17\%, n}$	Discounted Cash Flows	Cumulative Discounted Cash Flows
0	−$10,000	1.0	−$10,000	−$10,000
1	6,000	.855	5,130	−4,870
2	4,000	.731	2,924	−1,946
3	3,000	.624	1,872	−74
4	2,000	.534	1,068	994
5	1,000	.456	456	1,450

Project B

Year	Undiscounted Cash Flows	$PVIF_{17\%, n}$	Discounted Cash Flows	Cumulative Discounted Cash Flows
0	−$10,000	1.0	−$10,000	−$10,000
1	5,000	.855	4,275	−5,725
2	5,000	.731	3,655	−2,070
3	0	.624	0	−2,070
4	0	.534	0	−2,070
5	0	.456	0	−2,070

by this problem in selecting a maximum desired payback period. Moreover, as we will soon see, the net present value criterion is theoretically superior and no more difficult to calculate.

Although these deficiencies limit the value of the payback period and discounted payback period as tools for investment evaluation, these methods do have several positive features. First, they deal with cash flows, as opposed to accounting profits, and therefore focus on the true timing of the project's benefits and costs, even though the traditional payback period does not adjust the cash flows for the time value of money. Second, they are easy to visualize, quickly understood, and easy to calculate. Finally, although the payback period and discounted payback period methods have serious deficiencies, they are often used as rough screening devices to eliminate projects whose returns do not materialize until later years. These methods emphasize the earliest returns, which in all likelihood are less uncertain, and provide for the liquidity needs of the firm. Although their advantages are certainly significant, their disadvantages severely limit their value as discriminating capital-budgeting criteria.

BACK TO THE FUNDAMENTALS

The final three capital-budgeting criteria all incorporate **Axiom 2: The Time Value of Money—A Dollar Received Today Is Worth More than a Dollar Received in the Future** in their calculations. If we are at all to make rational business decisions we must recognize that money has a time value. In examining the following three capital-budgeting techniques you will notice that this axiom is the driving force behind each of them.

Net Present Value

The **net present value** (NPV) of an investment proposal is equal to the present value of its annual net cash flows after tax less the investment's initial outlay. The net present value can be expressed as follows:

$$NPV = \sum_{t=1}^{n} \frac{ACF_t}{(1 + k)^t} - IO \qquad (9\text{--}1)$$

where ACF_t = the annual after-tax cash flow in time period t (this can take on either positive or negative values)

k = the appropriate discount rate that is; the required rate of return or cost of capital[2]

IO = the initial cash outlay

n = the project's expected life

The project's net present value gives a measurement of the *net value* of an investment proposal in terms of today's dollars. Because all

---

[2]The required rate of return or cost of capital is the rate of return necessary to justify raising funds to finance the project or, alternatively, the rate of return necessary to maintain the firm's current market price per share. These terms will be defined in greater detail in Chapter 11.

cash flows are discounted back to the present, comparing the difference between the present value of the annual cash flows and the investment outlay does not violate the time value of money assumption. The difference between the present value of the annual cash flows and the initial outlay determines the net value of accepting the investment proposal in terms of today's dollars. Whenever the project's NPV is greater than or equal to zero, we will accept the project; and whenever there is a negative value associated with the acceptance of a project, we will reject the project. If the project's net present value is zero, then it returns the required rate of return and should be accepted. This accept-reject criterion is illustrated below:

$$\text{NPV} \geq 0.0: \text{ Accept}$$
$$\text{NPV} < 0.0: \text{ Reject}$$

The following example illustrates the use of the net present value capital-budgeting criterion.

EXAMPLE

A firm is considering new machinery, for which the after-tax cash flows are shown in Table 9–3. If the firm has a 12 percent required rate of return, the present value of the after-tax cash flows is $47,678, as calculated in Table 9–4. Furthermore, the net present value of the new machinery is $7,678. Because this value is greater than zero, the net present value criterion indicates that the project should be accepted. ■

Note that the worth of the net present value calculation is a function of the accuracy of cash flow predictions. Before the NPV criterion can reasonably be applied, incremental costs and benefits must first be estimated, including the initial outlay, the differential flows over the project's life, and the terminal cash flow.

The NPV criterion is the capital budgeting decision tool we will find most favorable for several reasons. First of all, it deals with cash flows rather than accounting profits. In this regard it is sensitive to the true timing of the benefits resulting from the project. Moreover, recognizing the time value of money allows comparison of the benefits and costs in a logical manner. Finally, because projects are accepted only if a positive net present value is associated with them, the acceptance of a project using this criterion will increase the value of the firm, which is consistent with the goal of maximizing the shareholders' wealth.

TABLE 9–3
NPV Illustration of
Investment in New
Machinery

	After-Tax Cash Flow
Initial outlay	–$40,000
Inflow year 1	15,000
Inflow year 2	14,000
Inflow year 3	13,000
Inflow year 4	12,000
Inflow year 5	11,000

	After-Tax Cash Flow	Present Value Factor at 12 Percent	Present Value
Inflow year 1	15,000	.893	$13,395
Inflow year 2	14,000	.797	11,158
Inflow year 3	13,000	.712	9,256
Inflow year 4	12,000	.636	7,632
Inflow year 5	11,000	.567	6,237
Present value of cash flows			$47,678
Investment initial outlay			−40,000
Net present value			$7,678

TABLE 9–4
Calculation for NPV
Illustration of Investment
in New Machinery

CALCULATOR SOLUTION³

Data Input	Function Key
40,000	+/− INPUT
15,000	INPUT
14,000	INPUT
13,000	INPUT
12,000	INPUT
11,000	INPUT
	EXIT CALC
12	I% YR

Function Key	Answer
NPV	7674.63

³If you are using an HP 17BII, first get to the CFLO menu and be certain that you have already cleared all prior data entries, selected both the "END MODE" and "one payment per year" (1P/YR), and turned the # times prompting (#T?) off. For further explanation see Appendix A.

The disadvantage of the NPV method stems from the need for detailed, long-term forecasts of the incremental cash flows accruing from the project's acceptance. Despite this drawback, the net present value is the most theoretically correct criterion that we will examine. The following example provides an additional illustration of its application.

EXAMPLE

A firm is considering the purchase of a new computer system, which will cost $30,000 initially, to aid in credit billing and inventory management. The incremental after-tax cash flows resulting from this project are provided in Table 9–5. The required rate of return demanded by the firm is 10 percent. To determine the system's net present value, the three-year $15,000 cash flow annuity is first discounted back to the present at 10 percent. From Appendix E in the back of this book, we find that $PVIFA_{10\%, 3 yr}$ is 2.487. Thus, the present value of this $15,000 annuity is $37,305.

Because the cash inflows have been discounted back to the present, they can now be compared with the initial outlay. This is because both of the flows are now stated in terms of today's dollars. Subtracting the initial outlay ($30,000) from the present value of the cash inflows ($37,305), we find that the system's net present value is $7,305. Because the NPV on this project is positive, the project should be accepted. ∎

	After-Tax Cash Flow
Initial outlay	−$30,000
Inflow Year 1	15,000
Inflow Year 2	15,000
Inflow Year 3	15,000

TABLE 9–5
NPV Example Problem of
Computer System

Profitability Index (Benefit/Cost Ratio)

The **profitability index** (PI), or **benefit/cost ratio,** is the ratio of the present value of the future net cash flows to the initial outlay. Although the net present value investment criterion gives a measure of the absolute dollar desirability of a project, the profitability index provides a relative measure of an investment proposal's desirability—that is, the ratio of the present value of its future net benefits to its initial cost. The profitability index can be expressed as follows:

$$PI = \frac{\sum_{t=1}^{n} \dfrac{ACF_t}{(1 + k)^t}}{IO} \qquad (9\text{--}2)$$

where ACF_t = the annual after-tax cash flow in time period t (this can take on either positive or negative values)

k = the appropriate discount rate; that is, the required rate of return or cost of capital

IO = the initial cash outlay

n = the project's expected life

The decision criterion with respect to the profitability index is to accept the project if the PI is greater than or equal to 1.00, and to reject the project if the PI is less than 1.00.

PI ≥ 1.0: Accept
PI < 1.0: Reject

Looking closely at this criterion, we see that it yields the same accept-reject decision as does the net present value criterion. Whenever the present value of the project's net cash flows is greater than its initial cash outlay, the project's net present value will be positive, signaling a decision to accept. When this is true, then the project's profitability index will also be greater than 1, as the present value of the net cash flows (the PI's numerator) is greater than its initial outlay (the PI's denominator). Although these two decision criteria will always yield the_ same decision, they will not necessarily rank acceptable projects in the same order. This problem of conflicting ranking will be dealt with at a later point.

Because the net present value and profitability index criteria are essentially the same, they have the same advantages over the other criteria examined. Both employ cash flows, recognize the timing of the cash flows, and are consistent with the goal of maximization of shareholders' wealth. The major disadvantage of this criterion, similar to the net present value criterion, is that it requires long, detailed cash flow forecasts.

EXAMPLE

A firm with a 10 percent required rate of return is considering investing in a new machine with an expected life of six years. The after-tax cash flows resulting from this investment are given in Table 9–6. Discounting the project's future net cash flows back to the present yields a present

TABLE 9–6
PI Illustration of Investment
in New Machinery

	After-Tax Cash Flow
Initial outlay	–$50,000
Inflow year 1	15,000
Inflow year 2	8,000
Inflow year 3	10,000
Inflow year 4	12,000
Inflow year 5	14,000
Inflow year 6	16,000

value of $53,667; dividing this value by the initial outlay of $50,000 gives a profitability index of 1.0733, as shown in Table 9–7. This tells us that the present value of the future benefits accruing from this project is 1.0733 times the level of the initial outlay. Because the profitability index is greater than 1.0, the project should be accepted. ∎

Internal Rate of Return

The **internal rate of return (IRR)** attempts to answer this question: What rate of return does this project earn? For computational purposes, the internal rate of return is defined as the discount rate that equates the present value of the project's future net cash flows with the project's initial cash outlay. Mathematically, the internal rate of return is defined as the value *IRR* in the following equation:

	After-Tax Cash Flow	Present Value Factor at 10 Percent	Present Value
Initial outlay	–$50,000	1.000	–$50,000
Inflow year 1	15,000	0.909	13,635
Inflow year 2	8,000	0.826	6,608
Inflow year 3	10,000	0.751	7,510
Inflow year 4	12,000	0.683	8,196
Inflow year 5	14,000	0.621	8,694
Inflow year 6	16,000	0.564	9,024

$$PI = \frac{\sum_{t=1}^{n} \dfrac{ACF_t}{(1+k)^t}}{IO}$$

$$= \frac{\$13,635 + \$6,608 + \$7,510 + \$8,196 + \$8,694 + \$9,024}{\$50,000}$$

$$= \frac{\$53,667}{\$50,000}$$

$$= 1.0733$$

$$IO = \sum_{t=1}^{n} \frac{ACF_t}{(1 + IRR)^t} \qquad (9\text{--}3)$$

where ACF_t = the annual after-tax cash flow in time period t (this can take on either positive or negative values)

IO = the initial cash outlay

n = the project's expected life

IRR = the project's internal rate of return

In effect, the IRR is analogous to the concept of the yield to maturity for bonds, which was examined in Chapter 6. In other words, a project's internal rate of return is simply the rate of return that the project earns.

The decision criterion associated with the internal rate of return is to accept the project if the internal rate of return is greater than or equal to the required rate of return. We reject the project if its internal rate of return is less than this required rate of return. This accept-reject criterion is illustrated below:

$IRR \geq$ required rate of return: Accept

$IRR <$ required rate of return: Reject

If the internal rate of return on a project is equal to the shareholders' required rate of return, then the project should be accepted. This is because the firm is earning the rate that its shareholders are requiring. However, the acceptance of a project with an internal rate of return below the investors' required rate of return will decrease the firm's stock price.

If the NPV is positive, then the IRR must be greater than the required rate of return, k. Thus, all the discounted cash flow criteria are consistent and will give similar accept-reject decisions. In addition, because the internal rate of return is another discounted cash flow criterion, it exhibits the same general advantages and disadvantages as both the net present value and profitability index, but has an additional disadvantage of being tedious to calculate if a financial calculator is not available.

Computing the IRR with a Financial Calculator

With today's calculators, the determination of an internal rate of return is merely a matter of a few keystrokes. In Chapter 5, whenever we were solving time value of money problems for i, we were really solving for the internal rate of return. For instance, in the example on page 156, when we solved for the rate that $100 must be compounded annually for it to grow to $179.10 in 10 years, we were actually solving for that problem's internal rate of return. Thus, with financial calculators we need only input the initial outlay, the cash flows and their timing, and then input the function key *I% YR* or the **IRR** button to calculate the internal rate of return.

Computing the IRR for Even Cash Flows

In this section we are going to put our calculators aside and examine the mathematical process of calculating internal rates of return for a better understanding of the IRR.

The calculation of a project's internal rate of return can either be very simple or relatively complicated. As an example of a straightforward solution, assume that a firm with a required rate of return of 10 percent is considering a project that involves an initial outlay of $45,555. If the investment is taken, the after-tax cash flows are expected to be $15,000 per annum over the project's four-year life. In this case, the internal rate of return is equal to IRR in the following equation:

$$\$45,555 = \frac{\$15,000}{(1 + IRR)^1} + \frac{\$15,000}{(1 + IRR)^2} + \frac{\$15,000}{(1 + IRR)^3} + \frac{\$15,000}{(1 + IRR)^4}$$

From our discussion of the present value of an annuity in Chapter 5, we know that this equation can be reduced to

$$\$45,555 = \$15,000 \left[\sum_{t=1}^{4} \frac{1}{(1 + IRR)^t} \right]$$

Appendix E gives values for the PVIFA $_{i,n}$ for various combinations of i and n, which further reduces this equation to

$$\$45,555 = \$15,000\ (PVIFA_{i,\ 4\ yr})$$

Dividing both sides by $15,000, this becomes

$$3.037 = PVIFA_{i,\ 4\ yr}$$

Hence, we are looking for PVIFA $_{i,\ 4\ yr}$ of 3.037 in the four-year row of Appendix E. This value occurs when i equals 12 percent, which means that 12 percent is the internal rate of return for the investment. Therefore, since 12 percent is greater than the 10 percent required return, the project should be accepted.

Computing the IRR for Uneven Cash Flows

Unfortunately, although solving for the IRR is quite easy when using a financial calculator or spreadsheet, it can be solved directly in the tables only when the future after-tax net cash flows are in the form of an annuity or a single payment. With a calculator the process is simple: One need only key in the initial cash outlay, the cash flows and theirtiming, and press the **IRR** button. When a financial calculator is not available and these flows are in the form of an uneven series of flows, a trial-and-error approach is necessary. To do this, we first determine the present value of the future after-tax net cash flows using an arbitrary discount rate. If the present value of the future cash flows at this discount rate is larger than the initial outlay, the rate is increased; if it is smaller than the initial outlay, the discount rate is lowered and the process begins again. This search routine is continued until the present value of the future after-tax cash flows is equal to the initial outlay. The interest rate that creates this situation is the internal rate of return. This is the same basic process that a financial calculator uses to calculate an IRR.

CALCULATOR SOLUTION[4]

Data Input	Function Key
45,555	+/– INPUT
15,000	INPUT
15,000	INPUT
15,000	INPUT
15,000	INPUT
	EXIT CALC

Function Key	Answer
IRR	12.01

[4]If you are using an HP 17BII, first get to the CFLO menu and be certain that you have already cleared all prior data entries, selected both the "END MODE" and "one payment per year" (1P/YR), and turned the # times prompting (#T?) off. For further explanation see Appendix A.

To illustrate the procedure, consider an investment proposal that requires an initial outlay of $3,817 and returns $1,000 at the end of year 1, $2,000 at the end of year 2, and $3,000 at the end of year 3. In this case, the internal rate of return must be determined using trial and error. This process is presented in Table 9–8, in which an arbitrarily selected discount rate of 15 percent was chosen to begin the process. The trial-and-error technique slowly centers in on the project's internal rate of return of 22 percent. The project's internal rate of return is then compared with the firm's required rate of return, and if the *IRR* is the larger, the project is accepted.

TABLE 9–8
Computing IRR for Uneven Cash Flows Without a Financial Calculator

Initial outlay	–$3,817
Inflow year 1	1,000
Inflow year 2	2,000
Inflow year 3	3,000

Solution:

Step 1: Pick an arbitrary discount rate and use it to determine the present value of the inflows.

Step 2: Compare the present value of the inflows with the initial outlay; if they are equal you have determined the IRR.

Step 3: If the present value of the inflows is larger (less than) than the initial outlay, raise (lower) the discount rate.

Step 4: Determine the present value of the inflows and repeat Step 2.

CALCULATOR SOLUTION[5]

Data Input	Function Key
3817	+/– INPUT
1000	INPUT
2000	INPUT
3000	INPUT
	EXIT CALC

Function Key	Answer
IRR%	21.98

[5]If you are using an HP 17BII, first get to the CFLO menu and be certain that you have already cleared all prior data entries, selected both the "END MODE" and "one payment per year" (1P/YR), and turned the # times prompting (#T?) off. For further explanation see Appendix A.

1. Try i = 15 percent:

	Net Cash Flows	Present Value Factor at 15 Percent	Present Value
Inflow year	$1,000	.870	$ 870
Inflow year 2	2,000	.756	1,512
Inflow year 3	3,000	.658	1,974
Present value of inflows			$4,356
Initial outlay			–$3,817

2. Try i = 20 percent:

	Net Cash Flows	Present Value Factor at 20 Percent	Present Value
Inflow year 1	$1,000	.833	$ 833
Inflow year 2	2,000	.694	1,388
Inflow year 3	3,000	.579	1,737
Present value of inflows			$3,958
Initial outlay			–$3,817

3. Try i = 22 percent:

	Net Cash Flows	Present Value Factor at 22 Percent	Present Value
Inflow year 1	$1,000	.820	$ 820
Inflow year 2	2,000	.672	1,344
Inflow year 3	3,000	.551	1,653
Present value of inflows			$3,817
Initial outlay			–$3,817

EXAMPLE

A firm with a required rate of return of 10 percent is considering three investment proposals. Given the information in Table 9–9, management plans to calculate the internal rate of return for each project and determine which projects should be accepted.

Because project A is an annuity, we can easily calculate its internal rate of return by determining the $PVIFA_{i,\,4\,yr}$ necessary to equate the present value of the future cash flows with the initial outlay. This computation is done as follows:

$$IO = \sum_{t=1}^{n} \frac{ACF_t}{(1 + IRR)^t}$$

$$\$10{,}000 = \sum_{t=1}^{4} \frac{\$3{,}362}{(1 + IRR)^t}$$

$$\$10{,}000 = \$3{,}362\,(PVIFA_{i,\,4\,yr})$$

$$2.974 = (PVIFA_{i,\,4\,yr})$$

We are looking for a $PVIFA_{i,\,4\,yr}$ of 2.974, in the four-year row of Appendix E, which occurs in the $i = 13$ percent column. Thus, 13 percent is the internal rate of return. Because this rate is greater than the firm's required rate of return of 10 percent, the project should be accepted.

Project B involves a single future cash flow of \$13,605, resulting from an initial outlay of \$10,000; thus, its internal rate of return can be determined directly from the present-value table in Appendix C as follows:

$$IO = \frac{ACF_t}{(1 + IRR)^t}$$

$$\$10{,}000 = \frac{\$13{,}605}{(1 + IRR)^4}$$

$$\$10{,}000 = \$13{,}605\,(PVIF_{i,\,4\,yr})$$

$$.735 = (PVIF_{i,\,4\,yr})$$

This tells us that we should look for a $PVIF_{i,\,4\,yr}$ of .735 in the four-year row of Appendix C, which occurs in the $i = 8$ percent column. We may therefore conclude that 8 percent is the internal rate of return. Because this rate is less than the firm's required rate of return of 10 percent, project B should be rejected.

TABLE 9–9
Three IRR Investment Proposal Examples

	A	B	C
Initial outlay	\$10,000	\$10,000	\$10,000
Inflow year 1	3,362	0	1,000
Inflow year 2	3,362	0	3,000
Inflow year 3	3,362	0	6,000
Inflow year 4	3,362	13,605	7,000

CAPITAL-BUDGETING TECHNIQUES AND PRACTICE

279

TABLE 9–10
Computing IRR for Project C

Try i = 15 percent:

	Net Cash Flows	Present Value Factor at 15 Percent	Present Value
Inflow year 1	$1,000	.870	$ 870
Inflow year 2	3,000	.756	2,268
Inflow year 3	6,000	.658	3,948
Inflow year 4	7,000	.572	4,004
Present value of inflows			$11,090
Initial outlay			–$10,000

Try i = 20 percent:

	Net Cash Flows	Present Value Factor at 20 Percent	Present Value
Inflow year 1	$1,000	.833	$ 833
Inflow year 2	3,000	.694	2,082
Inflow year 3	6,000	.579	3,474
Inflow year 4	7,000	.482	3,374
Present value of inflows			$ 9,763
Initial outlay			–$10,000

Try i = 19 percent:

	Net Cash Flows	Present Value Factor at 19 Percent	Present Value
Inflow year 1	$1,000	.840	$ 840
Inflow year 2	3,000	.706	2,118
Inflow year 3	6,000	.593	3,558
Inflow year 4	7,000	.499	3,493
Present value of inflows			$10,009
Initial outlay			–$10,000

CALCULATOR SOLUTION[6]

Data Input	Function Key
10,000	+/– INPUT
1000	INPUT
3000	INPUT
6000	INPUT
7000	INPUT
	EXIT CALC

Function Key	Answer
IRR%	19.04

[6]If you are using an HP 17BII, first get to the CFLO menu and be certain that you have already cleared all prior data entries, selected both the "END MODE" and "one payment per year" (1P/YR), and turned the # times prompting (#T?) off. For further explanation see Appendix A.

The uneven nature of the future cash flows associated with project C necessitates the use of the trial-and-error method. The internal rate of return for project C is equal to the value of *IRR* in the following equation:

$$\$10,000 = \frac{\$1,000}{(1 + IRR)^1} + \frac{\$3,000}{(1 + IRR)^2} + \frac{\$6,000}{(1 + IRR)^3} + \frac{\$7,000}{(1 + IRR)^4} \quad \text{(9–4)}$$

Arbitrarily selecting a discount rate of 15 percent and substituting it into equation (9–4) for IRR reduces the right-hand side of the equation to $11,090, as shown in Table 9–10. Therefore, because the present value of the future cash flows is larger than the initial outlay, we must raise the discount rate to find the project's internal rate of return. Substituting 20 percent for the discount rate, the right-hand side of equation (9–4) now becomes $9,763. As this is less than the initial outlay of $10,000, we must now decrease the discount rate. In other words, we know that the internal rate of return for this project is between 15 and 20 percent. Because the present value of the future flows discounted back to present at 20 percent was only $237 too low, a discount rate of 19 percent is selected. As shown in Table 9–10, a discount rate of 19 percent reduces the present value of the future inflows down to $10,009, which is approximately the same as the initial outlay. Consequently, project C's internal rate of return is approximately 19 percent.[7] Because the internal rate of return is greater than the firm's required rate of return of 10 percent, this investment should be accepted. ∎

Complications with IRR: Multiple Rates of Return

Although any project can have only one NPV and one PI, a single project under certain circumstances can have more than one IRR. The reason for this can be traced to the calculations involved in determining the IRR. Equation (9–3) states that the IRR is the discount rate that equates the present value of the project's future net cash flows with the project's initial outlay:

$$IO = \sum_{t=1}^{n} \frac{ACF_t}{(1 + IRR)^t} \qquad (9\text{–}3)$$

However, because equation (9–3) is a polynomial of a degree n, it has n solutions. Now if the initial outlay (IO) is the only negative cash flow and all the annual after-tax cash flows (ACF_t) are positive, then all but one of these n solutions is either a negative or imaginary number and there is no problem. But problems occur when there are sign reversals in the cash flow stream; in fact there can be as many solutions as there are sign reversals. Thus, a normal pattern with a negative initial outlay and positive annual after-tax cash flows after that (–, +, +, +, ... , +) has only one sign reversal, hence only one positive IRR. However, a pattern with more than one sign reversal can have more than one IRR. Consider, for example, the following pattern of cash flows.[8]

	After-Tax Cash Flow
Initial outlay	–$ 1,600
Year 1	+$ 10,000
Year 2	–$ 10,000

In this pattern of cash flows there are two sign reversals, from – $1,600 to + $10,000 and then from + $10,000 to – $10,000, so there can

---

[7]If desired, the actual rate can be more precisely approximated through interpolation as follows:

Discount Rate	Present Value		
19%	$10,009 ⎫	difference $9 ⎫	
IRR	10,000 ⎬		difference $246
20%	9,763 ⎭	⎭	

Thus, IRR = 19% + ($9/246)·1% = 19.04%

[8]This example is taken from James H. Lorie and Leonard J. Savage, "Three Problems in Rationing Capital," *Journal of Business* 28 (October 1955), pp. 229–39.

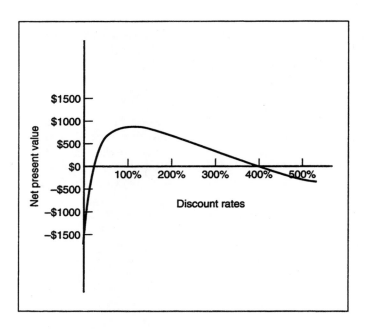

FIGURE 9–1
Multiple IRRs

be as many as two positive IRRs that will make the present value of the future cash flows equal to the initial outlay. In fact two internal rates of return solve this problem, 25 and 400 percent. Graphically what we are solving for is the discount rate that makes the project's NPV equal to zero; as Figure 9–1 illustrates, this occurs twice.

Which solution is correct? The answer is that neither solution is valid. Although each fits the definition of IRR, neither provides any insight into the true project returns. In summary, when there is more than one sign reversal in the cash flow stream, the possibility of multiple IRRs exists, and the normal interpretation of the IRR loses its meaning.

■ CAPITAL RATIONING

The use of our capital-budgeting decision rules developed in this chapter implies that the size of the capital budget is determined by the availability of acceptable investment proposals. However, a firm may place a limit on the dollar size of the capital budget. This situation is called **capital rationing.** As we will see, an examination of capital rationing will not only enable us to deal with complexities of the real world better but will serve to demonstrate the superiority of the NPV method over the IRR method for capital budgeting as well.

Using the internal rate of return as the firm's decision rule, a firm accepts all projects with an internal rate of return greater than the firm's required rate of return. This rule is illustrated in Figure 9–2, where projects A through E would be chosen. However, when capital rationing is imposed, the dollar size of the total investment is limited by the budget constraint. In Figure 9–2 the budget constraint of $X

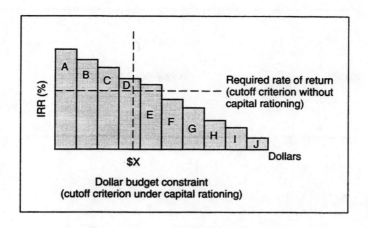

FIGURE 9–2
Projects Ranked by IRR

precludes the acceptance of an attractive investment, project E. This situation obviously contradicts prior decision rules. Moreover, the solution of choosing the projects with the highest internal rate of return is complicated by the fact that some projects may be indivisible; for example, it is meaningless to recommend that half project D be acquired.

PERSPECTIVE IN FINANCE

It is always somewhat uncomfortable to deal with problems associated with capital rationing because, under capital rationing, projects with positive net present values are rejected. This is a situation that violates the firm's goal of shareholder wealth maximization. However, in the real world capital rationing does exist, and managers must deal with it. Often when firms impose capital constraints they are recognizing that they do not have the ability to handle more than a certain number or dollar value of new projects profitably.

Rationale for Capital Rationing

We will first ask why capital rationing exists and whether it is rational. In general, three principal reasons are given for imposing a capital-rationing constraint. First, management may think market conditions are temporarily adverse. In the period surrounding the stock market crash of 1987 this reason was frequently given. At that time interest rates were high, and stock prices were depressed. Second, there may be a shortage of qualified managers to direct new projects; this can happen when projects are of a highly technical nature. Third, there may be intangible considerations. For example, management may simply fear debt, wishing to avoid interest payments at any cost. Or perhaps issuance of common stock may be limited to maintain a stable dividend policy.

Despite strong evidence that capital rationing exists in practice, the question remains as to its effect on the firm. In brief, the effect is negative, and to what degree depends on the severity of the rationing. If the rationing is minor and short-lived, the firm's share price will not suffer

		Profitability	Net Present
Project	Initial Outlay	Index	Value
A	$200,000	2.4	$280,000
B	200,000	2.3	260,000
C	800,000	1.7	560,000
D	300,000	1.3	90,000
E	300,000	1.2	60,000

TABLE 9-11
Capital-Rationing Example of Five Indivisible Projects

to any great extent. In this case capital rationing can probably be excused, although it should be noted that any capital rationing that rejects projects with positive net present values is contrary to the firm's goal of maximization of shareholders' wealth. If the capital rationing is a result of the firm's decision to limit dramatically the number of new projects or to limit total investment to internally generated funds, then this policy will eventually have a significantly negative effect on the firm's share price. For example, a lower share price will eventually result from lost competitive advantage if, owing to a decision to limit arbitrarily its capital budget, a firm fails to upgrade its products and manufacturing process.

Capital Rationing and Project Selection

If the firm decides to impose a capital constraint on investment projects, the appropriate decision criterion is to select the set of projects with the highest net present value subject to the capital constraint. This guideline may preclude merely taking the highest-ranked projects in terms of the profitability index or the internal rate of return. If the projects shown in Figure 9–2 are divisible, the last project accepted may be only partially accepted. Although partial acceptances may be possible in some cases, the indivisibility of most capital investments prevents it. If a project is a sales outlet or a truck, it may be meaningless to purchase half a sales outlet or half a truck.

To illustrate this procedure, consider a firm with a budget constraint of $1 million and five indivisible projects available to it, as given in Table 9–11. If the highest-ranked projects were taken, projects A and B would be taken first. At that point there would not be enough funds available to take project C; hence, projects D and E would be taken. However, a higher total net present value is provided by the combination of projects A and C. Thus projects A and C should be selected from the set of projects available. This illustrates our guideline: to select the set of projects that maximizes the firm's net present value.

Project Ranking

In the past, we have proposed that all projects with a positive net present value, a profitability index greater than 1.0, or an internal rate of return greater than the required rate of return be accepted, assuming there is no capital rationing. However, this acceptance is not always possible. In some cases, when two projects are judged acceptable by the discounted cash flow criteria, it may be necessary to select only one of them, as they are mutually exclusive. **Mutually exclusive projects** occur when a set of investment proposals perform essentially the same task; acceptance of one will necessarily mean rejection of the others. For example, a company considering the installation of a computer system may evaluate three or four systems, all of which may have positive net present values; however, the acceptance of one system will automatically mean rejection of the others. In general, to deal with mutually exclusive projects, we will simply rank them by means of the discounted cash flow criteria and select the project with the highest ranking. On occasion, however, problems of conflicting ranking may arise. As we will see, in general the net present value method is the preferred decision-making tool because it leads to the selection of the project that increases shareholder wealth the most.

Problems in Project Ranking

There are three general types of ranking problems: the size disparity problem, the time disparity problem, and the unequal lives problem. Each involves the possibility of conflict in the ranks yielded by the various discounted cash flow capital-budgeting criteria. As noted previously, when one discounted cash flow criterion gives an accept signal, they will all give an accept signal, but they will not necessarily rank all projects in the same order. In most cases this disparity is not critical; however, for mutually exclusive projects the ranking order is important.

Size Disparity

The *size disparity problem* occurs when mutually exclusive projects of unequal size are examined. This problem is most easily clarified with an example.

EXAMPLE

Suppose a firm is considering two mutually exclusive projects, A and B, both with required rates of return of 10 percent. Project A involves a $200 initial outlay and cash inflow of $300 at the end of one year, whereas project B involves an initial outlay of $1,500 and a cash inflow of $1,900 at the end of one year. The net present value, profitability index, and internal rate of return for these projects are given in Table 9–12.

In this case, if the net present value criterion is used, project B should be accepted, whereas if the profitability index or the internal rate of return criterion is used, project A should be chosen. The question now becomes: Which project is better? The answer depends on whether capital rationing exists. Without capital rationing, project B is better because it provides the largest increase in shareholders' wealth; that is, it has a larger net present value. If there is a capital constraint, the problem then focuses on what can be done with the additional $1,300 that is freed if project A is chosen (costing $200, as opposed to $1,500). If the firm can earn more on project A plus the project financed with the additional

TABLE 9–12 Size Disparity Ranking Problem		

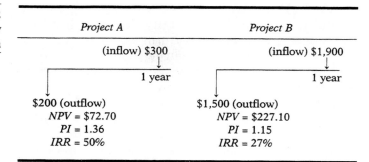

Project A	Project B
(inflow) $300	(inflow) $1,900
1 year	1 year
$200 (outflow)	$1,500 (outflow)
NPV = $72.70	NPV = $227.10
PI = 1.36	PI = 1.15
IRR = 50%	IRR = 27%

$1,300 than it can on project B, then project A and the marginal project should be accepted. In effect, we are attempting to select the set of projects that maximize the firm's NPV. Thus, if the marginal project has a net present value greater than $154.40 ($277.10 – $72.70), selecting it plus project A with a net present value of $72.70 will provide a net present value greater than $227.10, the net present value for project B. ■

In summary, whenever the size disparity problem results in conflicting rankings between mutually exclusive projects, the project with the largest net present value will be selected, provided there is no capital rationing. When capital rationing exists, the firm should select the set of projects with the largest net present value.

Time Disparity

The *time disparity problem* and the conflicting rankings that accompany it result from the differing reinvestment assumptions made by the net present value and internal rate of return decision criteria. The NPV criterion assumes that cash flows over the life of the project can be reinvested at the required rate of return or cost of capital, whereas the IRR criterion implicitly assumes that the cash flows over the life of the project can be reinvested at the internal rate of return. Again, this problem may be illustrated through the use of an example.

EXAMPLE

Suppose a firm with a required rate of return or cost of capital of 10 percent and with no capital constraint is considering the two mutually exclusive projects illustrated in Table 9–13. The net present value and profitability index indicate that project A is the better of the two, whereas the internal rate of return indicates that project B is the better. Project B receives its cash flows earlier than project A, and the different assumptions made as to how these flows can be reinvested result in the difference in rankings. Which criterion should be followed depends on which reinvestment assumption is used. The net present value criterion is preferred in this case because it makes the most acceptable assumption for the wealth-maximizing firm. It is certainly the most conservative assumption that can be made, because the required rate of return is the lowest possible reinvestment rate. Moreover, as we have already

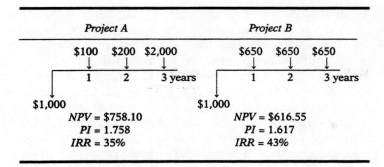

TABLE 9–13
Time Disparity Ranking
Problem

noted, the net present value method maximizes the value of the firm and the shareholders' wealth. ∎

Unequal Lives

The final ranking problem to be examined centers on the question of whether it is appropriate to compare mutually exclusive projects with different life spans.

EXAMPLE

Suppose a firm with a 10 percent required rate of return is faced with the problem of replacing an aging machine and is considering two replacement machines, one with a three-year life and one with a six-year life. The relevant cash flow information for these projects is given in Table 9–14.

Examining the discounted cash flow criteria, we find that the net present value and profitability index criteria indicate that project B is the better project, whereas the internal rate of return favors project A. This ranking inconsistency is caused by the different life spans of the projects being compared. In this case the decision is a difficult one because the projects are not comparable.

The problem of incomparability of projects with different lives arises because future profitable investment proposals may be rejected without

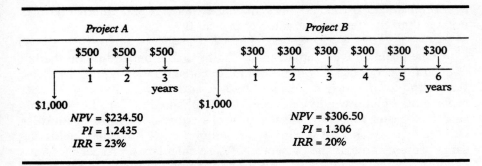

TABLE 9–14
Unequal Lives Ranking
Problem

being included in the analysis. This can easily be seen in a replacement problem such as the present example, in which two mutually exclusive machines with different lives are being considered. In this case a comparison of the net present values alone on each of these projects would be misleading. If the project with the shorter life were taken, at its termination the firm could replace the machine and receive additional benefits, whereas acceptance of the project with the longer life would exclude this possibility, a possibility that is not included in the analysis. The key question thus becomes: Does today's investment decision include all future profitable investment proposals in its analysis? If not, the projects are not comparable. In this case, if project B is taken, then the project that could have been taken after three years when project A terminates is automatically rejected without being included in the analysis. Thus, acceptance of project B not only forces rejection of project A, but also forces rejection of any replacement machine that might have been considered for years 4 through 6 without including this replacement machine in the analysis.

There are several methods to deal with this situation. The first option is to assume that the cash inflows from the shorter-lived investment will be reinvested at the required rate of return until the termination of the longer-lived asset. Although this approach is the simplest, merely calculating the net present value, it actually ignores the problem at hand—that of allowing for participation in another replacement opportunity with a positive net present value. The proper solution thus becomes the projection of reinvestment opportunities into the future— that is, making assumptions about possible future investment opportunities. Unfortunately, while the first method is too simplistic to be of any value, the second is extremely difficult, requiring extensive cash flow forecasts. The final technique for confronting the problem is to assume that reinvestment opportunities in the future will be similar to the current ones. The two most common ways of doing this are by creating a replacement chain to equalize life spans or calculating the project's Equivalent Annual Annuity (EAA). Using a replacement chain, the present example would call for the creation of a two-chain cycle for project A; that is, we assume that project A can be replaced with a similar investment at the end of three years. Thus, project A would be viewed as two A projects occurring back to back, as illustrated in Figure 9–3. The net present value on this replacement chain is $426.50, which is comparable with project B's net present value. Therefore, project A should be accepted because the net present value of its replacement chain is greater than the net present value of project B.

One problem with replacement chains is that depending on the life of each project, it can be quite difficult to come up with equivalent lives. For example, if the two projects had 7- and 13-year lives, a 91-year replacement chain would be needed to establish equivalent lives. In this case it is easier to determine the project's **equivalent annual annuity (EAA).** A project's EAA is simply an annuity cash flow that yields the same present value as the project's NPV. To calculate a project's EAA we need only calculate a project's NPV and then divide that number by the

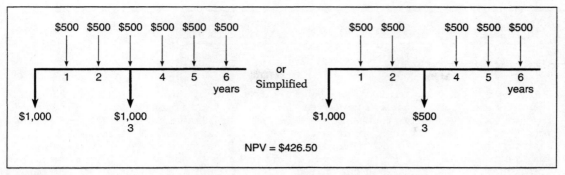

FIGURE 9–3
Replacement Chain Illustration: Two A Project A's Back to Back

$PVIFA_{i,n}$ to determine the dollar value of an n-year annuity that would produce the same NPV as the project. This can be done in two steps as follows:

Step 1: *Calculate the project's NPV.* In Table 9–14 we determined that project A had an NPV of $234.50, whereas project B had an NPV of $306.50.

Step 2: *Calculate the EAA.* The EAA is determined by dividing each project's NPV by the $PVIFA_{i,n}$ where i is the required rate of return and n is the project's life. This determines the level of an annuity cash flow that would produce the same NPV as the project. For project A the $PVIFA_{10\%, 3\ yr}$ is equal to 2.487, whereas the $PVIFA_{10\%, 6\ yr}$ for project B is equal to 4.355. Dividing each project's NPV by the appropriate $PVIFA_{i,n}$ we determine the EAA for each project:

$$EAA_A = NPV/PVIFA_{i,n}$$
$$= \$234.50/2.487$$
$$= \$94.29$$
$$EAA_B = \$306.50/4.355$$
$$= \$70.38$$

How do we interpret the EAA? For a project with an n-year life, it tells us what the dollar value is of an n-year annual annuity that would provide the same NPV as the project. Thus, for project A it means that a three-year annuity of $94.29 given a discount rate of 10 percent would produce a net present value the same as project A's net present value, which is $234.50. We can now compare the equivalent annual annuities directly to determine which project is better. We can do this because we now have found the level of annual annuity that produces an NPV equivalent to the project's NPV. Thus, because they are both annual annuities they are comparable. An easy way to see this is to use the EAAs to create infinite-life replacement chains. To do this we need only calculate the present value of an infinite stream or perpetuity of equivalent annual annuities. This is done by using the present value of an

CAPITAL-BUDGETING
TECHNIQUES
AND PRACTICE

289

infinite annuity formula, that is, simply dividing the equivalent annual annuity by the appropriate discount rate. In this case we find:

$$NPV_{\infty, A} = \$94.29/.10$$
$$= \$942.90$$
$$NPV_{\infty, B} = \$70.38/.10$$
$$= \$703.80$$

Here we have calculated the present value of an infinite-life replacement chain. Because the EAA method provides the same results as the infinite-life replacement chain, it really doesn't matter which method you prefer to use. ∎

ETHICS IN CAPITAL BUDGETING

Although it may not seem obvious, ethics has a role in capital budgeting. Beech-Nut provides an example of how these rules have been violated in the past and what the consequences can be. No doubt this project appeared to have a positive net present value associated with it, but in fact, it cost Beech-Nut tremendously. The *Ethics in Financial Management* insert, "Bad Apple for Baby," tells what occurred.

BACK TO THE FUNDAMENTALS

Ethics and ethical considerations continually crop up when capital-budgeting decisions are being made. This brings us back to **Axiom 9: Ethical Behavior Is Doing the Right Thing, and Ethical Dilemmas Are Everywhere in Finance.** As the *Ethics in Financial Management* insert, "Bad Apple for Baby," points out, the most damaging event a business can experience is a loss of the public's confidence in its ethical standards. In making capital-budgeting decisions we must be aware of this, and that ethical behavior is doing the right thing and is the right thing to do.

A GLANCE AT ACTUAL CAPITAL-BUDGETING PRACTICES

During the past 35 years the popularity of each of the capital-budgeting methods has shifted rather dramatically. In the 1950s the payback period method dominated capital budgeting, but through the 1960s and 1970s the discounted cash flow decision techniques slowly displaced the nondiscounted techniques. This movement from the payback period to net present value and the internal rate of return is shown in Table 9–15, which indicates the growth in popularity of these techniques as reflected in surveys of practices over the years. Interestingly, although most firms use the NPV and IRR as their primary techniques, most firms also use the payback period as a secondary decision method for capital budgeting. In a sense they are using the payback period to control for risk. The logic behind this is that because the payback period dramatically emphasizes early cash flows, which are presumably more certain—that is, have less risk—than cash flows occurring later in a project's life, managers believe its use will lead to projects with more certain cash flows.

A reliance on the payback period came out even more dramatically in a study of the capital-budgeting practices of 12 large manufacturing firms.[9] Information for this study was gathered from interviews over one to three days in addition to an examination of the records of about 400 projects. This study revealed several points of interest. First, firms were typically found to categorize capital investments as mandatory (regulations and contracts, capitalized maintenance, replacement of antiqued

---

[9]Marc Ross, "Capital Budgeting Practices of Twelve Large Manufacturers," *Financial Management*, 15 (Winter 1986), pp. 15–22.

TABLE 9–15
Past Surveys of Capital-Budgeting Practices—Percent of Respondents Using Each Technique

Capital-Budgeting Technique	Klammer, 1959	Klammer, 1964	Klammer, 1970	Petty et al., 1972	Kim and Farragher, 1975	Gitman and Forrester, 1977	Kim and Farragher 1979	Kim, Crick and Kim 1986
Primary method:								
NPV	5%	15%	27%	15%	26%	13%	19%	21%
IRR	8	17	30	41	37	53	49	49
Payback	34	24	12	11	15	9	12	19
Secondary method:								
NPV	2%	3%	7%	14%	7%	28%	8%	24%
IRR	1	2	6	19	7	14	8	15
Payback	18	21	32	37	33	44	39	35

Sources: Thomas Klammer, "Empirical Evidence of the Adoption of Sophisticated Capital Budgeting Techniques," *Journal of Business* (July 1972), pp. 387–397; J. William Petty, David F. Scott, Jr., and Monroe M. Bird, "The Capital Expenditure Decision-Making Process of Large Corporations," *Engineering Economist* (Spring 1975), pp. 159–172; S. H. Kim and E. J. Farragher, "Capital Budgeting Practices in Large Industrial Firms," *Baylor Business Studies* (November 1976), pp. 19–25; Lawrence J. Gitman and John R. Forrester, Jr., "Forecasting and Evaluation Practices and Performance: A Survey of Capital Budgeting," *Financial Management* (Fall 1977), pp. 66–71; S. H. Kim and E. J. Farragher, "Current Capital Budgeting Practices," *Management Accounting* (June 1981), pp. 26–30; and Suk H. Kim, T. Crick, and Sesung H. Kim, "Do Executives Practice What Academics Preach?" *Management Accounting* (November 1986), pp. 49–52.

equipment, product quality) or discretionary (expanded markets, new businesses, cost cutting), with the decision-making process being different for mandatory and discretionary projects. Second, it was found that the decision-making process was different for projects of differing size. In fact, approval authority tended to rest in different locations, depending on the size of the project. Table 9–16 provides the typical levels of approval authority.

The study also showed that while the discounted cash flow methods are used at most firms, the simple payback criterion was the measure relied on primarily in one-third of the firms examined. The use of the payback period seemed to be even more common for smaller projects, with firms severely simplifying the discounted cash flow analysis or relying primarily on the payback period. Thus, although discounted cash flow decision techniques have become more widely accepted, their use depends to an extent on the size of the project and where within the firm the decision is being made.

TABLE 9–16
Project Size and Decision-Making Authority

Project Size	Typical Boundaries	Primary Decision Site
Very small	Up to $100,000	Plant
Small	$100,000 to $1,000,000	Division
Medium	$1 million to $10 million	Corporate investment committee
Large	Over $10 million	CEO & board

SUMMARY

The process of capital budgeting involves decision making with respect to investment in fixed assets. We examine four commonly used criteria for determining the acceptance or rejection of capital-budgeting proposals. The first method, the payback period, does not incorporate the time value of money into its calculations, although a variation of it, the discounted payback period, recognizes the time value of money. The discounted methods, the net present value, profitability index, and internal rate of return, do account for the time value of money. These methods are summarized in Table 9–17.

This chapter introduces several complications into the capital-budgeting process. First, we examine capital rationing and the problems it can create by imposing a limit on the dollar size of the capital budget. Although capital rationing does not, in general, lead to the goal of maximization of shareholders' wealth, it does exist in practice. We also discuss problems associated with the evaluation of mutually exclusive projects. Mutually exclusive projects occur when a set of investment proposals perform essentially the same task. In general, to deal with mutually exclusive projects, we rank them by means of the discounted cash flow criteria and select the project with the highest ranking. Conflicting rankings

---

TABLE 9–17
Capital-Budgeting Criteria

1. Payback period = number of years required to recapture the initial investment

Accept if payback ≤ maximum acceptable payback period
Reject if payback > maximum acceptable payback period

Advantages:
- Uses cash flows.
- Is easy to calculate and understand.
- May be used as rough screening device.

Disadvantages
- Ignores the time value of money.
- Ignores cash flows occurring after the payback period
- Selection of the maximum acceptable payback period is arbitrary.

2. Discounted Payback period--the number of years needed to recover the initial cash outlay from the *discounted net cash flows*.

Accept if discounted payback ≤ maximum acceptable discounted payback period
Reject if discounted payback > maximum acceptable discounted payback period

Advantages
- Uses cash flows.
- Is easy to calculate and understand.
- Consider time value of money

Disadvantages
- Ignores cash flows occurring after the payback period.
- Selection of the maximum acceptable payback period is arbitrary.

3. Net present value = present value of the annual cash flows after tax less the investment's initial outlay

$$NPV = \sum_{t=1}^{n} \frac{ACF_t}{(1+k)^t} - IO$$

where ACF_t = the annual after-tax cash flow in time period t (this can take on either positive or negative values)

k = the appropriate discount rate; that is, the required rate of return or the cost of capital

IO = the initial cash outlay

n = the project's expected life

Accept if $NPV \geq 0.0$
Reject if $NPV < 0.0$

Advantages:	Disadvantages:
• Uses cash flows.	• Requires detailed long-term forecasts of the incremental benefits and costs.
• Recognizes the time value of money.	
• Is consistent with the firm goal of shareholder wealth maximization.	

• Profitability index = the ratio of the present value of the future net cash flows to the initial outlay.

$$PI = \frac{\sum_{t=1}^{n} \dfrac{ACF_t}{(1+k)^t}}{IO}$$

Accept if $PI \geq 1.0$
Reject if $PI < 1.0$

Advantages:	Disadvantages:
• Uses cash flows.	• Requires detailed long-term forecasts of the incremental benefits and costs.
• Recognizes the time value of money.	
• Is consistent with the firm goal of shareholder wealth maximization.	

• Internal rate of return = the discount rate that equates the present value of the project's future net cash flows with the project's initial outlay.

$$IO = \sum_{t=1}^{n} \frac{ACF_t}{(1 + IRR)^t}$$

where IRR = the project's internal rate of return

Accept if $IRR \geq$ required rate of return
Reject if $IRR <$ required rate of return

Advantages:	Disadvantages:
• Uses cash flows.	• Requires detailed long-term forecasts of the incremental benefits and costs.
• Recognizes the time value of money.	
• Is in general consistent with the firm goal of shareholder wealth maximization.	• Can involve tedious calculations.
	• Possibility of multiple IRRs.

may arise because of the size disparity problem, the time disparity problem, and unequal lives. The problem of incomparability of projects with different lives is not simply a result of the different lives; rather, it arises because future profitable investment proposals may be rejected without being included in the analysis. Replacement chains and equivalent annual annuities are presented as possible solutions to this problem.

STUDY QUESTIONS

9–1.   Why is the capital-budgeting decision such an important process? Why are capital-budgeting errors so costly?

9–2.   What are the criticisms of the use of the payback period as a capital-budgeting technique? What are its advantages? Why is it so frequently used?

9–3.   In some countries, expropriation of foreign investments is a common practice. If you were considering an investment in one of those countries, would the use of the payback period criterion seem more reasonable than it otherwise might? Why?

9–4.   Briefly compare and contrast the NPV, PI and IRR criteria. What are the advantages and disadvantages of using each of these methods?

9–5.   What are mutually exclusive projects? Why might the existence of mutually exclusive projects cause problems in the implementation of the discounted cash flow capital-budgeting criteria?

9–6.   What are common reasons for capital rationing? Is capital rationing rational?

9–7.   How should managers compare two mutually exclusive projects of unequal size? Would your approach change if capital rationing existed?

9–8.   What causes the time disparity ranking problem? What reinvestment rate assumptions are associated with the net present value and internal rate of return capital-budgeting criteria?

9–9.   When might two mutually exclusive projects having unequal lives be incomparable? How should managers deal with this problem?

SELF-TEST PROBLEMS

ST-1.   You are considering a project that will require an initial outlay of $54,200. This project has an expected life of 5 years and will generate after-tax cash flows to the company as a whole of $20,608 at the end of each year over its five-year life. In addition to the $20,608 cash flow from operations during the fifth and final year, there will be an additional cash inflow of $13,200 at the end of the fifth year associated with the salvage value of the machine, making the cash flow in year 5 equal to $33,808. Thus the cash flows associated with this project look like this:

Year	Cash Flow
0	–$54,200
1	20,608
2	20,608
3	20,608
4	20,608
5	33,808

Given a required rate of return of 15 percent, calculate the following:

a. Payback Period
b. Net present value
c. Profitablility index
d. Internal rate of return
Should this project be accepted?

ST-2. The J. Serrano Corporation is considering signing a one-year contract with one of two computer-based marketing firms. Although one is more expensive, it offers a more extensive program and thus will provide higher after-tax net cash flows. Assume these two options are mutually exclusive and that the required rate of return is 12 percent. Given the following after-tax net cash flows:

Year	Option A	Option B
0	–$50,000	–$100,000
1	70,000	130,000

a. Calculate the net present value.
b. Calculate the profitability index.
c. Calculate the internal rate of return.
d. If there is no capital-rationing constraint, which project should be selected? If there is a capital-rationing constraint, how should the decision be made?

STUDY PROBLEMS

9–1. *(IRR Calculation)* Determine the internal rate of return on the following projects:
   a. An initial outlay of $10,000 resulting in a single cash flow of $17,182 after 8 years
   b. An initial outlay of $10,000 resulting in a single cash flow of $48,077 after 10 years
   c. An initial outlay of $10,000 resulting in a single cash flow of $114,943 after 20 years
   d. An initial outlay of $10,000 resulting in a single cash flow of $13,680 after 3 years

9–2. *(IRR Calculation)* Determine the internal rate of return on the following projects:
   a. An initial outlay of $10,000 resulting in a cash flow of $1,993 at the end of each year for the next 10 years
   b. An initial outlay of $10,000 resulting in a cash flow of $2,054 at the end of each year for the next 20 years
   c. An initial outlay of $10,000 resulting in a cash flow of $1,193 at the end of each year for the next 12 years
   d. An initial outlay of $10,000 resulting in a cash flow of $2,843 at the end of each year for the next 5 years

9–3. *(IRR Calculation)* Determine the internal rate of return to the nearest percent on the following projects:
   a. An initial outlay of $10,000 resulting in a cash flow of $2,000 at the end of year 1, $5,000 at the end of year 2, and $8,000 at the end of year 3
   b. An initial outlay of $10,000 resulting in a cash flow of $8,000 at the end of year 1, $5,000 at the end of year 2, and $2,000 at the end of year 3
   c. An initial outlay of $10,000 resulting in a cash flow of $2,000 at the end of years 1 through 5 and $5,000 at the end of year 6

9–4. *(NPV, PI, and IRR Calculations)* Fijisawa, Inc., is considering a major expansion of its product line and has estimated the following cash flows associated with such an expansion. The initial outlay associated with the expansion would be $1,950,000 and the project would generate incremental after-tax cash flows of $450,000 per year for six years. The appropriate required rate of return is 9 percent.
   a. Calculate the net present value.
   b. Calculate the profitability index.

c. Calculate the internal rate of return.

d. Should this project be accepted?

9–5. *(Payback Period, Net Present Value, Profitability Index, and Internal Rate of Return Calculations)* You are considering a project with an initial cash outlay of $80,000 and expected after-tax cash flows of $20,000 at the end of each year for 6 years. The required rate of return for this project is 10 percent.

a. What are the project's payback and discounted payback periods?

b. What is the project's NPV?

c. What is the project's PI?

d. What is the project's IRR?

9–6. *(Net Present Value, Profitability Index, and Internal Rate of Return Calculations)* You are considering two independent projects, Project A and Project B. The initial cash outlay associated with Project A is $50,000 and the initial cash outlay associated with Project B is $70,000. The required rate of return on both projects is 12 percent. The expected annual after-tax cash inflows from each project are as follows:

Year	Project A	Project B
0	$12,000	$13,000
1	12,000	13,000
2	12,000	13,000
3	12,000	13,000
4	12,000	13,000
5	12,000	13,000
6	12,000	13,000

Calculate the NPV, PI, and IRR for each project and indicate if the project should be accepted.

9–7. *(Payback Period Calculations)* You are considering three independent projects, Project A, Project B, and Project C. The required rate of return is 10 percent on each. Given the following cash flow information calculate the payback period and discounted payback period for each.

Year	Project A	Project B	Project C
0	–$1,000	–$10,000	–$5,000
1	600	5,000	1,000
2	300	3,000	1,000
3	200	3,000	2,000
4	100	3,000	2,000
5	500	3,000	2,000

If you require a 3-year payback for both the traditional and discounted payback period methods before an investment can be accepted, which projects would be accepted under each criterion?

9–8. *(NPV with Varying Required Rates of Return)* Dowling Sportswear is considering building a new factory to produce aluminum baseball bats. This project would require an initial cash outlay of $5,000,000 and will generate annual after-tax cash inflows of $1,000,000 per year for 8 years. Calculate the project's NPV given:

a. A required rate of return of 9 percent.

b. A required rate of return of 11 percent.

c. A required rate of return of 13 percent.

d. A required rate of return of 15 percent.

9–9.   (*Internal Rate of Return Calculations*) Given the following cash flows, determine the internal rate of return for the three independent projects A, B, and C.

	Project A	Project B	Project C
Initial Investment:	–$50,000	–$100,000	–$450,000
Cash Inflows:			
Year 1	$10,000	25,000	200,000
Year 2	15,000	25,000	200,000
Year 3	20,000	25,000	200,000
Year 4	25,000	25,000	–
Year 5	30,000	25,000	–

9–10.   (*NPV with Varying Required Rates of Return*) Big Steve's, makers of swizzle sticks, is considering the purchase of a new plastic stamping machine. This investment requires an initial outlay of $100,000 and will generate after-tax cash inflows of $18,000 per year for 10 years. For each of the listed required rates of return, determine the project's net present value.
   a. The required rate of return is 10 percent.
   b. The required rate of return is 15 percent.
   c. Would the project be accepted under part (a) or (b)?
   d. What is this project's internal rate of return?

9–11.   (*Size Disparity Ranking Problem*) The D. Dorner Farms Corporation is considering purchasing one of two fertilizer-herbicides for the upcoming year. The more expensive of the two is better and will produce a higher yield. Assume these projects are mutually exclusive and that the required rate of return is 10 percent. Given the following after-tax net cash flows:

Year	Project A	Project B
0	–$500	–$5,000
1	700	6,000

   a. Calculate the net present value.
   b. Calculate the profitability index.
   c. Calculate the internal rate of return.
   d. If there is no capital-rationing constraint, which project should be selected? If there is a capital-rationing constraint, how should the decision be made?

9–12.   (*Time Disparity Ranking Problem*) The State Spartan Corporation is considering two mutually exclusive projects. The cash flows associated with those projects are as follows:

Year	Project A	Project B
0	–$50,000	–$ 50,000
1	15,625	0
2	15,625	0
3	15,625	0
4	15,625	0
5	15,625	$100,000

The required rate of return on these projects is 10 percent.
a. What is each project's payback period?
b. What is each project's net present value?
c. What is each project's internal rate of return?
d. What has caused the ranking conflict?
e. Which project should be accepted? Why?

9–13. *(Unequal Lives Ranking Problem)* The B. T. Knight Corporation is considering two mutually exclusive pieces of machinery that perform the same task. The two alternatives available provide the following set of after-tax net cash flows:

Year	Equipment A	Equipment B
0	–$20,000	–$20,000
1	12,590	6,625
2	12,590	6,625
3	12,590	6,625
4		6,625
5		6,625
6		6,625
7		6,625
8		6,625
9		6,625

Equipment A has an expected life of three years, whereas equipment B has an expected life of nine years. Assume a required rate of return of 15 percent.
a. Calculate each project's payback period.
b. Calculate each project's net present value.
c. Calculate each project's internal rate of return.
d. Are these projects comparable?
e. Compare these projects using replacement chains and EAA. Which project should be selected? Support your recommendation.

9–14. *(EAAs)* The Andrzejewski Corporation is considering two mutually exclusive projects, one with a 3-year life and one with a 7-year life. The after-tax cash flows from the two projects are as follows:

Year	Project A	Project B
0	–$50,000	–$50,000
1	20,000	36,000
2	20,000	36,000
3	20,000	36,000
4	20,000	
5	20,000	
6	20,000	
7	20,000	

a. Assuming a 10 percent required rate of return on both projects, calculate each project's EAA. Which project should be selected?
b. Calculate the present value of an infinite-life replacement chain for each project.

9–15. *(Capital Rationing)* The Cowboy Hat Company of Stillwater, Okla., is considering seven capital investment proposals, for which the funds available are limited to a maximum of $12 million. The projects are independent and have the following costs and profitability indexes associated with them:

Project	Cost	Profitablitity Index
A	$4,000,000	1.18
B	3,000,000	1.08
C	5,000,000	1.33
D	6,000,000	1.31
E	4,000,000	1.19
F	6,000,000	1.20
G	4,000,000	1.18

a. Under strict capital rationing, which projects should be selected?
b. What problems are there with capital rationing?

SELF-TEST SOLUTIONS

SS-1:

a.
$$\text{Payback period} = \frac{\$54,200}{\$20,608} = 2.630 \text{ years}$$

b.
$$NPV = \sum_{t=1}^{n} \frac{ACF_t}{(1+k)^t} - IO$$

$$= \sum_{t=1}^{4} \frac{\$20,608}{(1+.15)^t} + \frac{\$33,808}{(1+.15)^5} - \$54,200$$

$$= \$20,608 \,(2.855) + \$33,808 \,(.497) - \$54,200$$

$$= \$58,836 + \$16,803 - \$54,200$$

$$= \$21,439$$

c.
$$PI = \frac{\sum_{t=1}^{n} \dfrac{ACF_t}{(1+k)^t}}{IO}$$

$$= \frac{\$75,639}{\$54,200}$$

$$= 1.396$$

d.
$$IO = \sum_{t=1}^{n} \frac{ACF_t}{(1+IRR)^t}$$

$$\$54,200 = \$20,608 \,(PVIFA_{IRR\%,\ 4\ yr}) + \$33,808 \,(PVIF_{IRR\%,\ 5\ yr})$$

Try 29 percent

$$\$54,200 = \$20,608 \,(2.203) + \$33,808 \,(.280)$$

$$= \$45,399 + 9,466$$

$$= \$54,865$$

Try 30 percent

$$\$45,200 = \$20,608 \,(2.166) + \$33,808 \,(.269)$$

$$= \$44,637 + 9,094$$

$$= \$53,731$$

Thus, the IRR is just below 30 percent and the project should be accepted because the NPV is positive, the PI is greater than 1.0, and the IRR is greater than the required rate of return of 15 percent.

SS-2.

a.

$$NPV_A = \$70,000 \left[\frac{1}{(1 + .12)^1} \right] - \$50,000$$

$$= \$70,000 \ (.893) - \$50,000$$

$$= \$62,510 - \$50,000$$

$$= \$12,510$$

$$NPV_B = \$130,000 \left[\frac{1}{(1 + .12)^1} \right] - \$100,000$$

$$= \$130,000 \ (.893) - \$100,000$$

$$= \$116,090 - \$100,000$$

$$= \$16,090$$

b.

$$PI_A = \frac{\$62,510}{\$50,000}$$

$$= 1.2502$$

$$PI_B = \frac{\$116,090}{\$100,000}$$

$$= 1.1609$$

c. $\$50,000 = \$70,000 \ (PVIF_{i, \ 1 \ yr})$

$.7143 = PVIF_{i, \ 1 \ yr}$

Looking for a value of $PVIF_{i, \ 1yr}$ in Appendix C, a value of .714 is found in the 40 percent column. Thus, the IRR is 40 percent.

$\$100,000 = \$130,000 \ (FVIF_{i, \ 1 \ yr})$

$.7692 = PVIF_{i, \ 1 \ yr}$

Looking for a value of $PVIF_{i, \ 1 \ yr}$ in Appendix C a value of .769 is found in the 30 percent column. Thus, the IRR is 30 percent.

d. If there is no capital rationing, project B should be accepted because it has a larger net present value. If there is a capital constraint, the problem focuses on what can be done with the additional $50,000 (the additional money that could be invested if project A, with an initial outlay of $50,000, were selected over project B, with an initial outlay of $100,000). In the capital constraint case, if Serrano can earn more on project A plus the marginal project financed with the additional $50,000 than it can on project B, then project A and the marginal project should be accepted.

Investing in Employee Productivity: An Application of Capital Budgeting
from ABC News, Business World, October 14, 1990

In the introduction to this video case we asked a list of pertinent questions. See Video Case 3 Introduction on page 266.

If the programs Fel-Pro implemented increase employee satisfaction, the firm could benefit in many ways. Lower employee turnover, lower absenteeism, and fewer job-related accidents and illnesses (which translate into lower health insurance claims) all reduce costs and thereby increase profits. If the firm ever comes on hard times, the loyalty built by these programs might allow the firm to ask for help from its employees in the form of lower raises, unpaid leaves, and so on.

Program costs are fairly easy to estimate. One problem with cost estimation in programs with volunteer participation is uncertainty about the number of employees who will participate. Once the program is opened to all employees, the firm must either be prepared to make sufficient opportunities available for all interested employees or explain how the resources will be rationed.

Arriving at quantitative estimates for the programs' benefits can be very difficult. One approach would be to estimate how much absenteeism and employee turnover costs the firm, then estimate how absenteeism and turnover are affected by the programs. The value of loyalty and commitment are much more difficult to measure.

In theory NPV analysis could be used to evaluate investments such as this, but the inability to quantify all future benefits makes applying NPV nearly impossible. Because the benefits are more difficult to value than the costs, strict application of NPV analysis may produce results that are biased against acceptance. Managers' primary commitment is to shareholders. If there are no benefits from implementing the employee incentive programs, they should not be implemented. Implementing costly programs that produce no benefits will eventually harm more groups than shareholders alone. If the firm becomes less competitive because of these extra costs, then employees may lose their jobs, and communities may lose factories. Although the objective of maximization of shareholder wealth appears, at first glance, to ignore the many other constituencies associated with a firm—employees, suppliers, customers, and the community—it is the only objective that assures the firm's long-term viability, and thereby the firm's continued support of its various constituents.

Discussion questions

1. Like employee morale, the benefits of adding personal computers to the workplace are difficult to estimate. What are some of the benefits from providing computers to employees and how might these benefits be estimated?

2. One form of employee benefit is training. However, as employees improve their skills or learn new skills, they become more attractive to competitors and may be hired away. Firms that provide training but experience high turnover bear costs but receive no benefits. How would you address this potential problem? Examples to consider are the extensive training programs offered by many banks. After 10 to 16 months of training, during which the employees-in-training have not been particularly productive for the bank, they are attractive to other banks or many corporations.

Suggested readings

FISHER, ANNE. "The Morale Crisis," *Fortune*, November 18, 1991.

KIRKPATRICK, DAVID. "Here Comes the Payoff from PCs," *Fortune*, November 18, 1991.

BASIC FINANCIAL MANAGEMENT
Frequently Used Symbols

α_t	Certainty equivalent coefficient in period t	MCC	Marginal cost of capital
ACF_t	Annual after-tax expected cash flow in time period t	MIRR	Modified internal rate of return
AROR	Accounting rate of return	NPV	Net present value
ß	Beta of an asset, the slope of the regression or characteristic line	PMT	Periodic level payment of an annuity
		P/E	Price/earnings ratio
DCL	Degree of combined leverage	PV	Present value
DFL	Degree of financial leverage	PVIF	Present value interest factor
DOL	Degree of operating leverage	PVIFA	Present value interest factor for an annuity
EAA	Equivalent annual annuity	R	Investor's required and/or expected rate of return
EBIT	Earnings before interest and taxes		
EOQ	Economic order quantity	R_f	Risk free rate of return
EPS	Earnings per share	ROA	Return on assets
FV	Future value	ROE	Return on common equity
FVIF	Future value interest factor	RP	Risk premium
FVIFA	Future value interest factor for an annuity	SML	Security market line
g	Annual growth rate	σ	Standard deviation (lowercase sigma)
IO	the initial cash outlay	σ^2	Variance (standard deviation squared)
IRR	Internal rate of return	TIE	Times interest earned
Kc	Cost of internal common equity (also Kc)	T	Tax rate
Kd	After-tax cost of debt	WCC	Weighted cost of capital
Ko	Weighted cost of capital	W_d, W_c	Percentage (weights) of funds provided by debt and common equity respectively
Kp	Cost of preferred stock		
M/B	Market-to-book ratio	YTM	Yield to maturity

Answers to Selected Questions

CHAPTER 4

4-1. Total Assets = $1.8 million

4-3. Total Assets = $2 million
Fixed Assets = $800,000
Inventories = $1 million

4-5.
Cash	NO
Marketable Securities	NO
Accounts Payable	YES
Notes Payable	NO
Plant and Equipment	NO
Inventories	YES

4-7. a. Notes Payable $1.11 million
b. Current Ratio (before) = 2 times
Current Ratio (after) = 1.12 times

4-9.

Cumulative Borrowing

Jan	Feb	March	April	May	June	July
0	0	$52,100	$96,721	$52,688	0	0

CHAPTER 9

9-1. a. IRR=7%
b. IRR=17%

9-3. a. IRR=approximately 19%

9-5. a. payback period = 4 years
discounted payback period = 5.37 years

9-7. a. Project A:
payback period = 2.5 years
discounted payback period = 3.84 years

9-11. a. NPV_A = $136.30
NPV_B = $455.
b. PI_A = 1.2726
PI_B = 1.09
c. IRR_A = 40%
IRR_B = 20%

9-13. a. Payback A = 1.589 years
Payback B = 3.019 years
b. NPV_A = $8,743
NPV_B = $11,615
c. IRR_A = 40%
IRR_B = 30%